Carving Caricature Bookmarks

A Beginner's Step-by-Step Guide

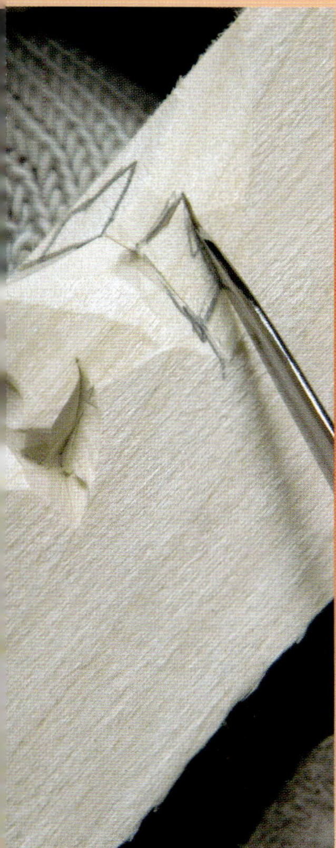

Chris Morgan

Schiffer Publishing Ltd®

4880 Lower Valley Road • Atglen, PA 19310

Dedication

I would like to thank my wife Amanda and daughter Avri, who support my carving, and Gregg Thompson, who got me started in carving.

Acknowledgments

A special *Thank You* to my wife Amanda for taking the photographs in this book.

Contents

Library of Congress Control Number: 2012934144

Designed by Mark David Bowyer
Type set in New Baskerville BT / Humanist521 BT

ISBN: 978-0-7643-4083-3
Printed in China

Schiffer Books are available at special discounts for bulk purchases for sales promotions or premiums. Special editions, including personalized covers, corporate imprints, and excerpts can be created in large quantities for special needs. For more information contact the publisher:

Published by Schiffer Publishing Ltd.
4880 Lower Valley Road
Atglen, PA 19310
Phone: (610) 593-1777; Fax: (610) 593-2002
E-mail: Info@schifferbooks.com

For the largest selection of fine reference books on this and related subjects,
please visit our website at: **www.schifferbooks.com**
We are always looking for people to write books on new and related subjects.
If you have an idea for a book, please contact us at:
proposals@schifferbooks.com

This book may be purchased from the publisher.
Please try your bookstore first.
You may write for a free catalog.

In Europe, Schiffer books are distributed by
Bushwood Books
6 Marksbury Ave.
Kew Gardens
Surrey TW9 4JF England
Phone: 44 (0) 20 8392 8585; Fax: 44 (0) 20 8392 9876
E-mail: info@bushwoodbooks.co.uk
Website: www.bushwoodbooks.co.uk

Introduction

A few years ago, when I was on my way back from vacation, I stopped at a theme park in Branson, Missouri. I had been there many times growing up and was always fascinated with the woodcarvers who were there demonstrating. In years past, I had always gone to the woodcarving shop and thought how nice it would be to start carving. This time I had a little help with making the decision. My wife decided that she had heard enough of me talking about starting and took it upon herself to ask one of the carvers there to sell me what I needed to start my own carvings. The carver demonstrating that day sold me the items I needed, gave me some blanks to practice with, and some pointers on knife safety. I took these items back home and the next day started carving. Almost instantaneously, I developed a passion for woodcarving. Now, I am constantly practicing, sketching new ideas, and talking to people about woodcarving that want to learn more about this art form.

Woodcarving has taught me a lot about myself and has given me a great appreciation for the people who practice this art. Woodcarving can also expose you to life-long friendships like the one that I have now with the carver who was demonstrating that day at the amusement park. I hope all of you who read this book develop skills that you can build on and keep you carving.

Chapter One

Basic Cuts and Safety

Before we begin, I would like to give you a brief description of the different types of cuts we will be using when we carve the bookmark. They are the STOP CUT, "V" CUT, PUSH CUT, and PEAR CUT.

The **STOP CUT** is the most basic cut of all and is made by plunging the knife straight into the wood at any given depth. This will allow you to remove wood up to this cut, preventing it from splitting or breaking above or below your stop cut line.

The **"V" CUT** is made by making a stop cut and then cutting towards the stop cut from both sides, removing the material and leaving you with a "v"-shape area. This cut can be used in various ways when we are carving the bookmarks.

The **PUSH CUT** is made with your thumb on the back of the blade when you are making a deep cut. This cut gives you the extra power you need to remove larger pieces of wood.

The **PEAR CUT** is just the opposite of the push cut. Just think of it as if you are peeling a pear cutting towards you — make sure your thumb is under the wood when you finish the cut.

The safety aspect of woodcarving is very important and sometimes beginning woodcarvers overlook it. Most carvers will use safety equipment that will prevent most cuts and stabs from their tools. The items will include a carving glove that is made of Kevlar® or stainless steel fibers woven into the glove and a leather thumb guard or carver's tape wrapped around the thumb of the knife hand. I would highly recommend a heavy weight-carving glove to give you the most protection from unwanted mishaps.

The main idea in woodcarving is to have fun and to stay safe. Pay close attention to knife and finger placement, grain of wood and how it reacts when making your cuts, soft spots in the wood that can cause breaks, and where the knife tip will travel when it does. All of these things are very important to keep yourself safe.

To make our stop cut, push the knife straight into the wood and make a straight cut. This is only one cut.

To make the push cut, hold the knife and with the opposite thumb on the back side of the blade push towards the stop cut.

The end result from making the stop cut and the push cut towards the stop cut.

To make a pear cut, the motion is just like peeling a pear. The thumb is below the cutting plane as you draw the knife back towards you to make the cut.

This is a "v" cut. It is made by starting with a stop cut and then a push cut towards the stop cut on either side of the stop cut.

Side view of the "v" cut. This cut will vary in depth and width.

Chapter 2

Carving the Eye

There are many different ways to carve a caricature eye. This detail look at the eye is how I carve a lot of my eyes, which makes it simple for beginners to learn. This chapter will be useful when we are carving the Santa bookmark and you'll need a more in-depth look at some of the steps we will be carving.

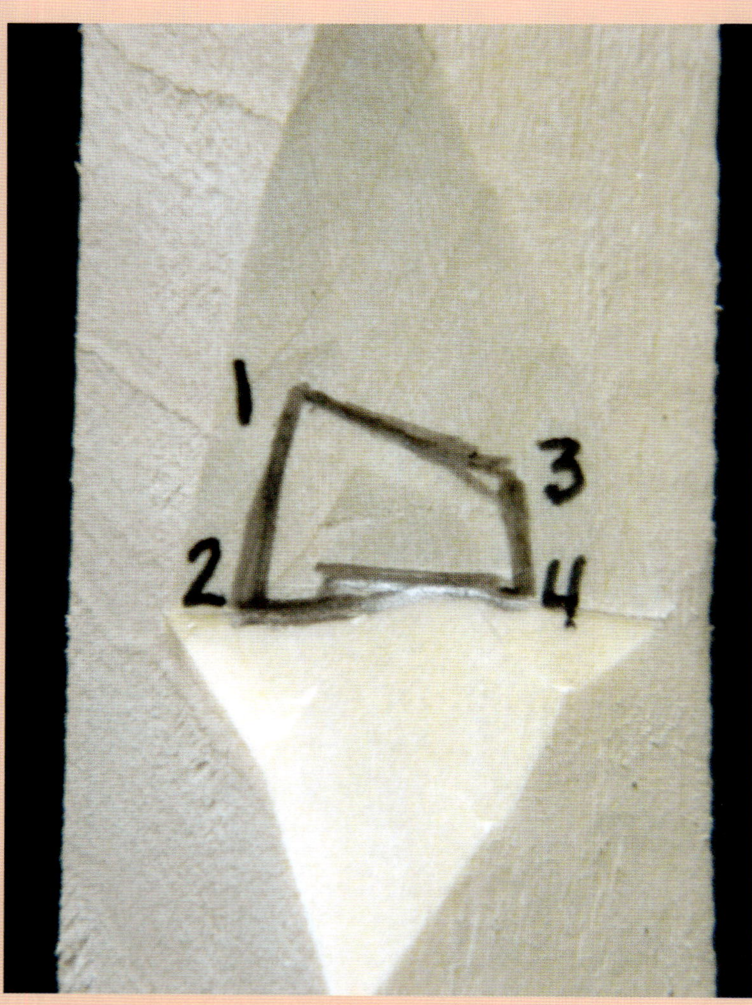

We have made a fairly wide "v" cut and have drawn a trapezoid shape that will be our eye. The numbers marked are the corners we will be removing.

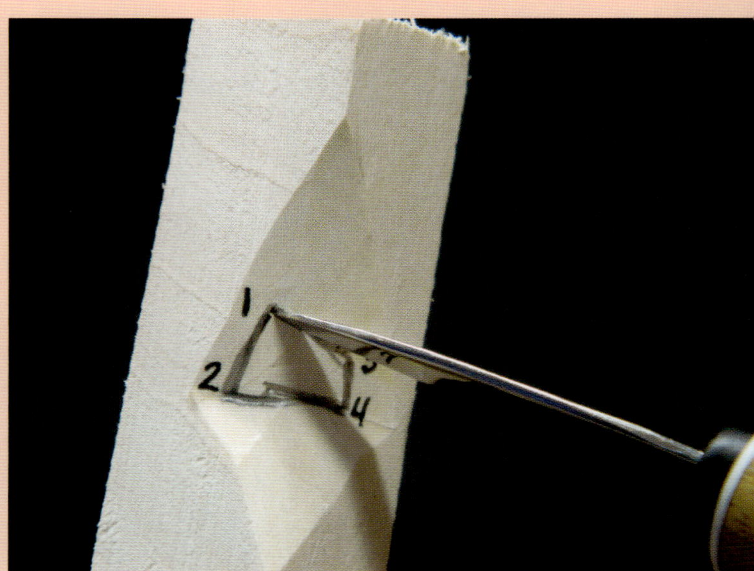

Start by making a stop cut on the line of "Corner 1" as shown about 1/8" deep.

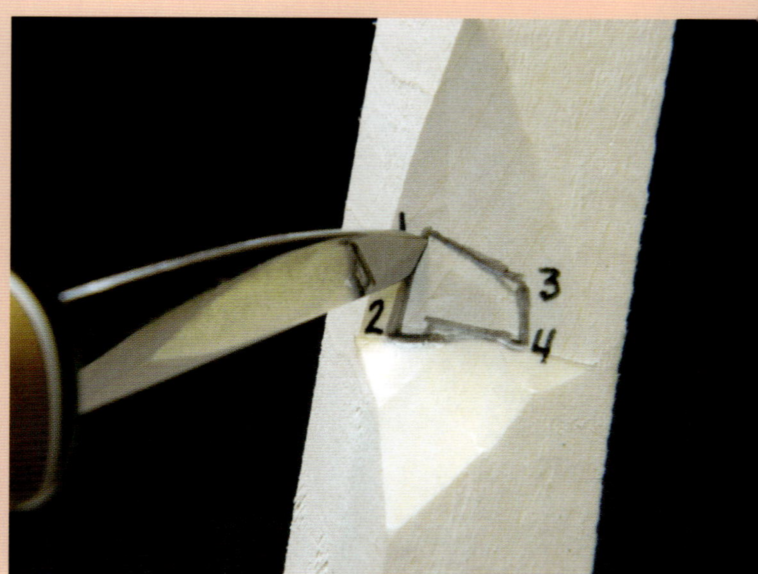

Now, on the other line of "corner 1," cut the same 1/8" depth as before.

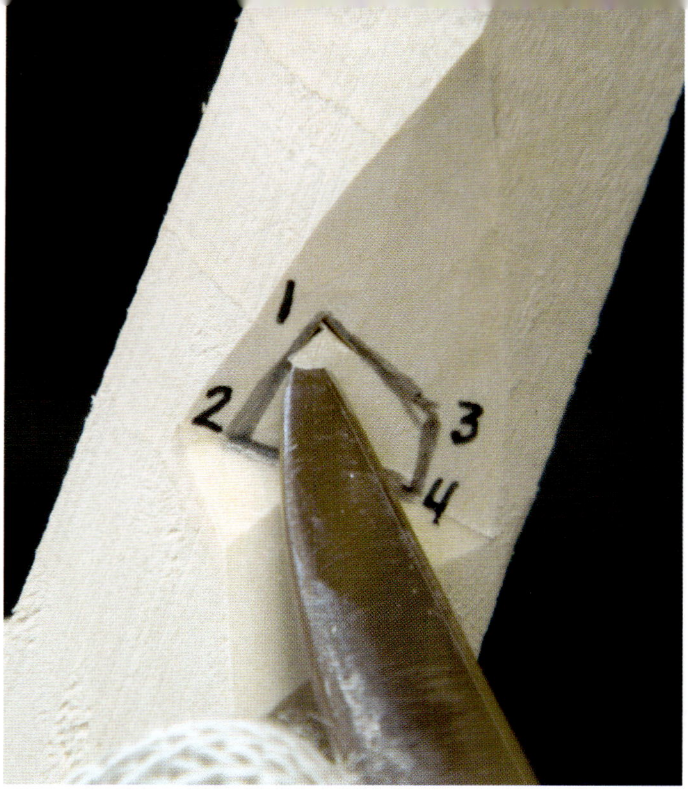

Cut diagonally from left to right connecting the two previous cuts.

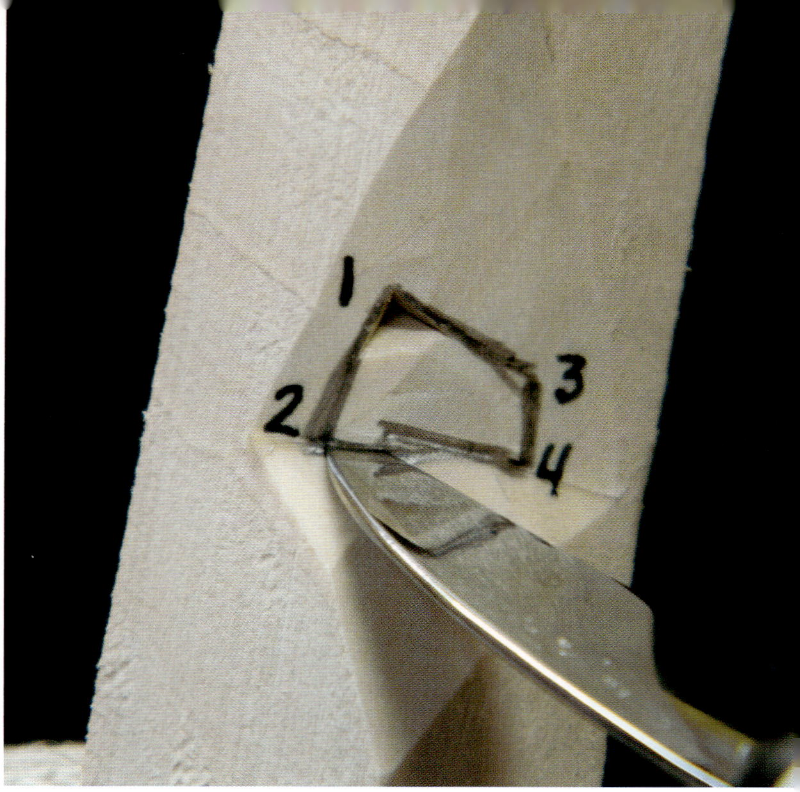

Repeat the process for all four corners.

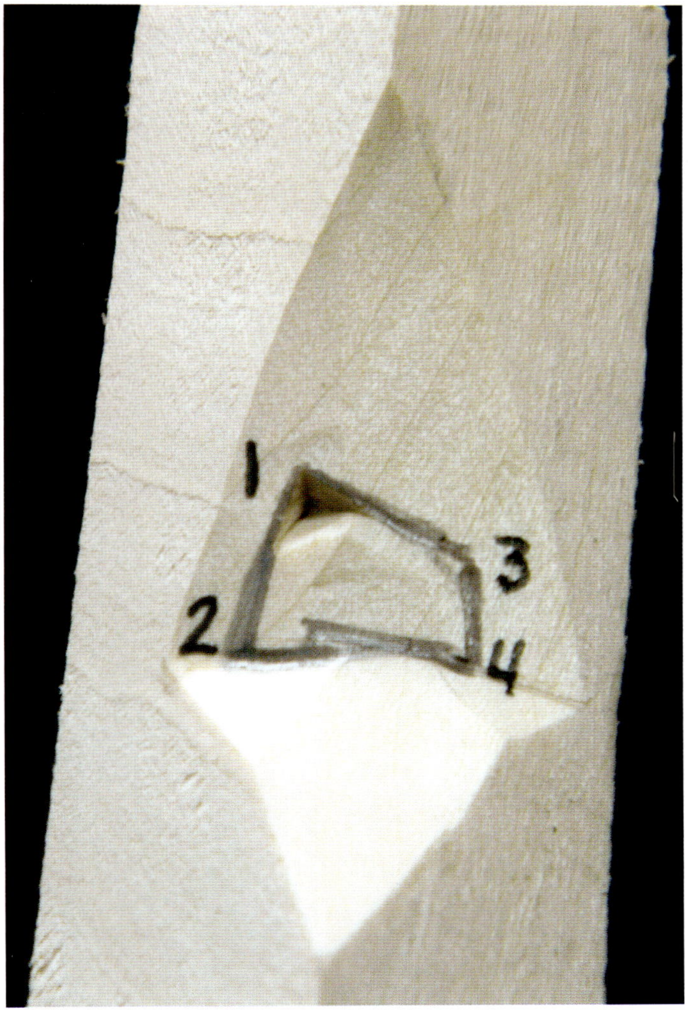

After the three cuts are made, the triangle piece will come out, leaving us with one corner done.

Corner 2 removed.

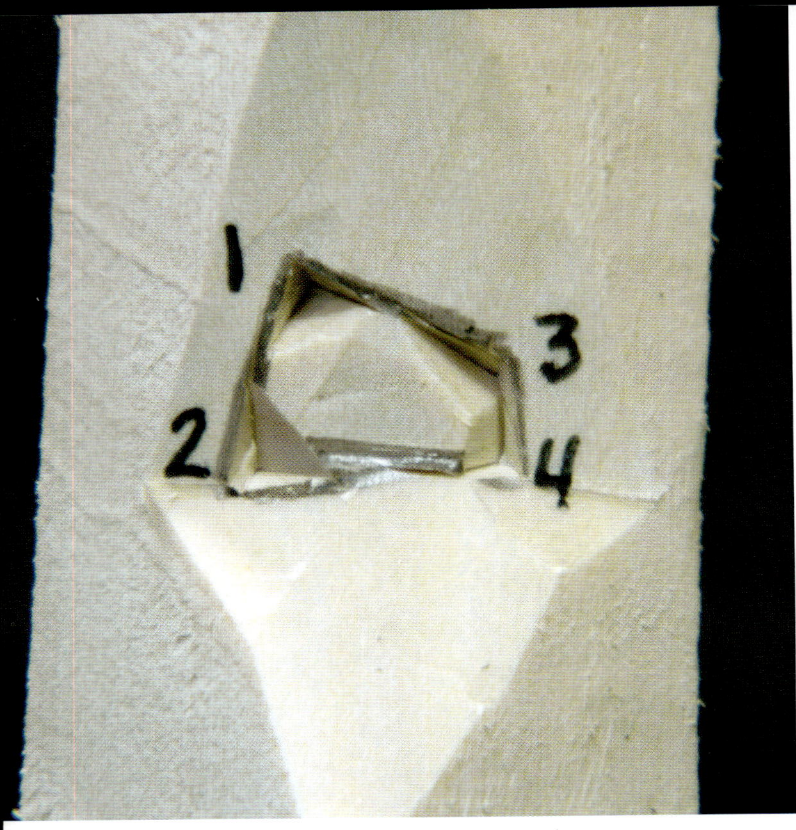

All four of the corners are removed, and the eyeball is now exposed.

Small diagonal cuts to round the corner of the eyeball. You will do this for all four corners.

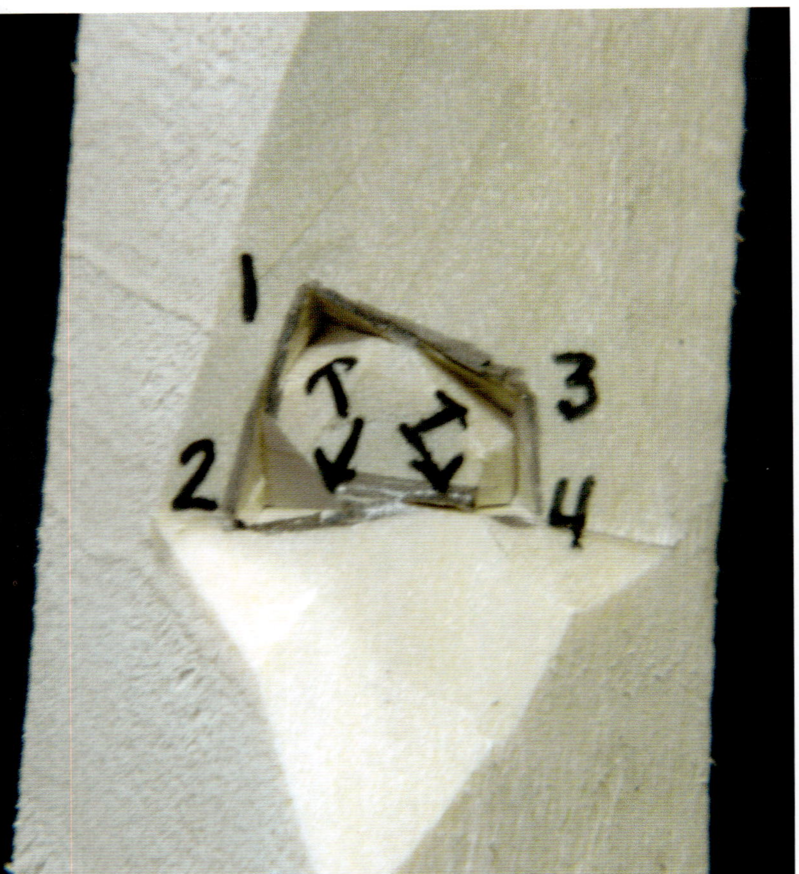

The arrows marked will be the direction in which we will be cutting to shape the eyeball.

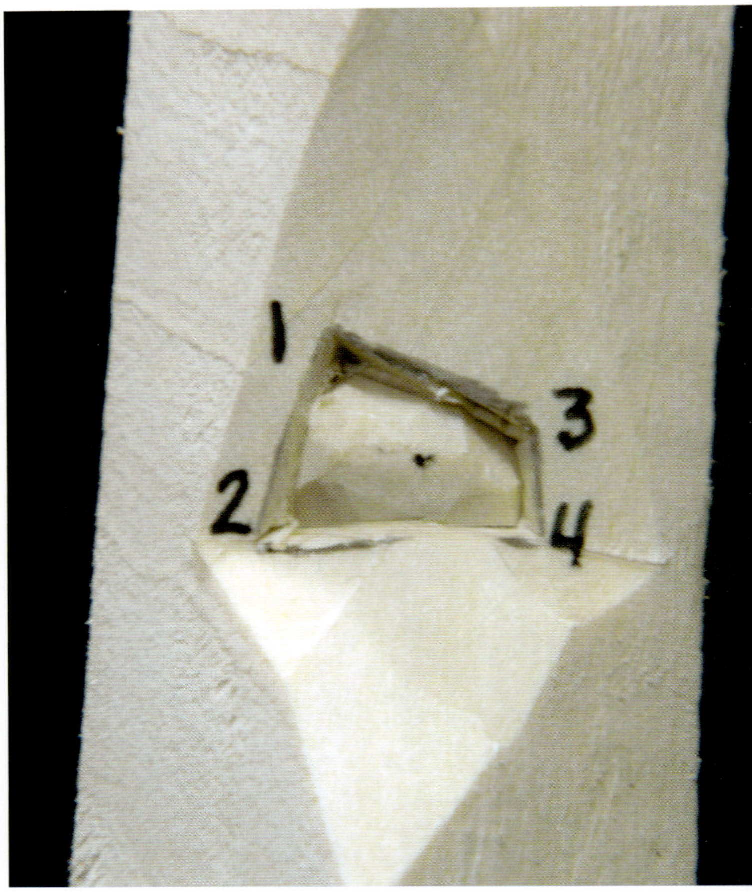

All four corners are now rounded off — the idea is to have the eyeball round with no flat areas.

The upper eyelid is now marked and we will use a small v-tool to create this cut along the marked line. This line has been marked approximately 1/8" above the eye.

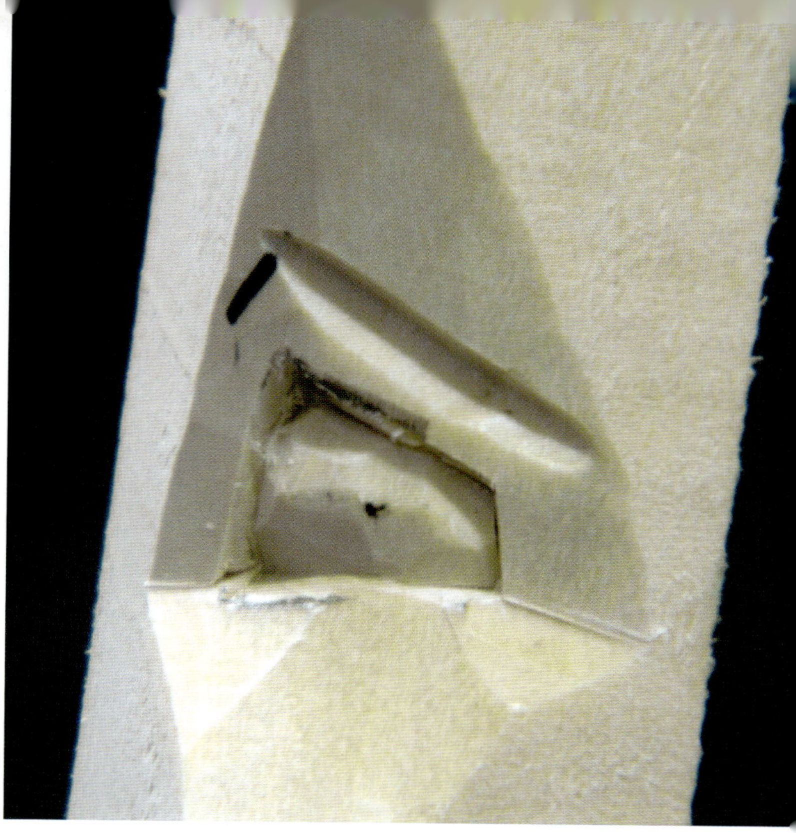

The first eyelid cut done; now make the same cut on the remaining line towards the previous cut.

Using the v-tool, start to cut on the line towards the top of the eyelid.

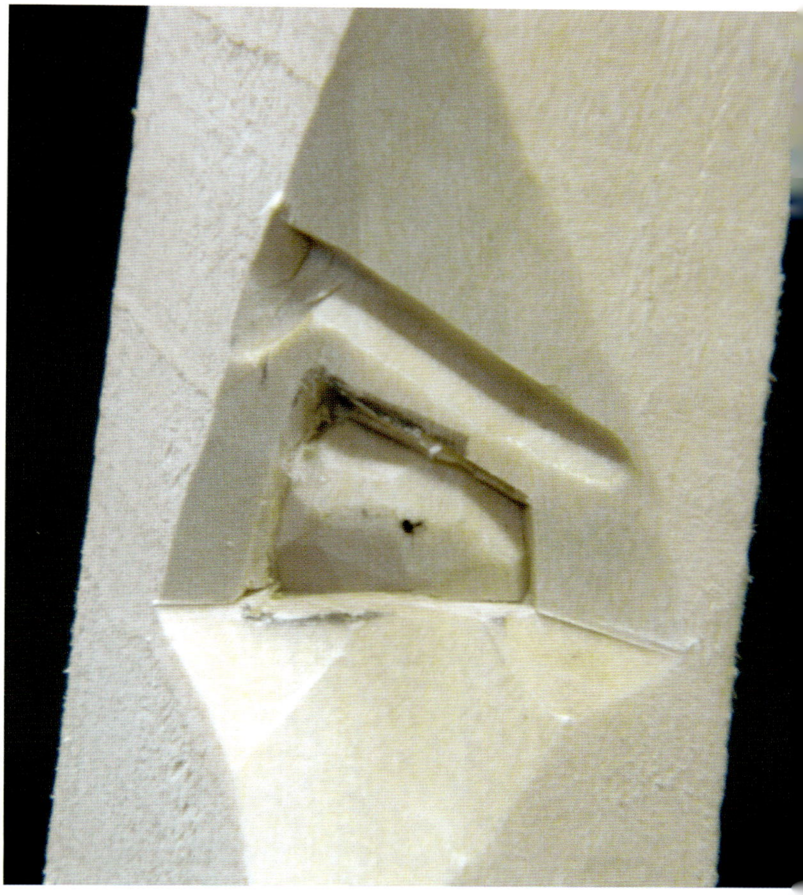

After making those cuts, the eyelid should look like this.

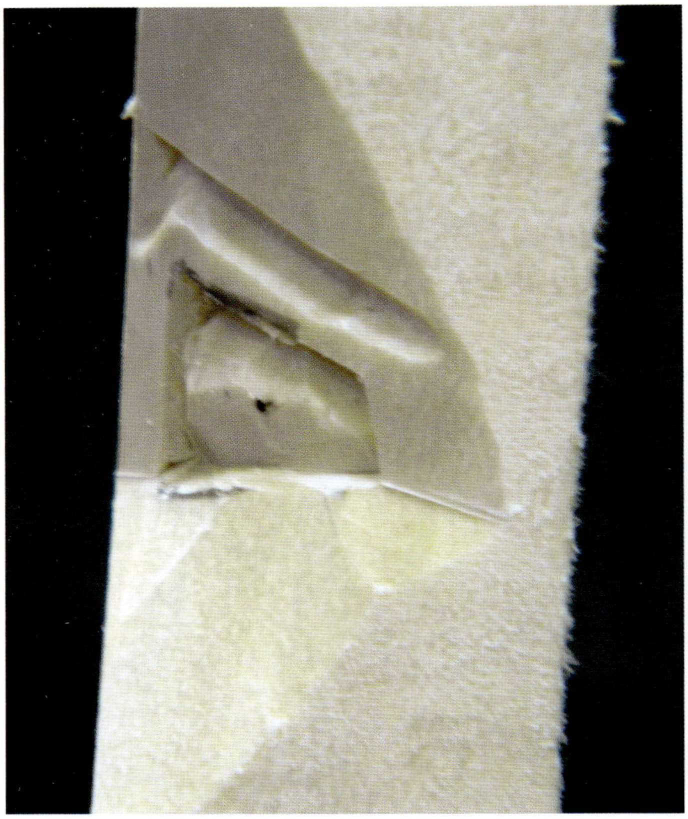

This is what the eyelid looks like from the side.

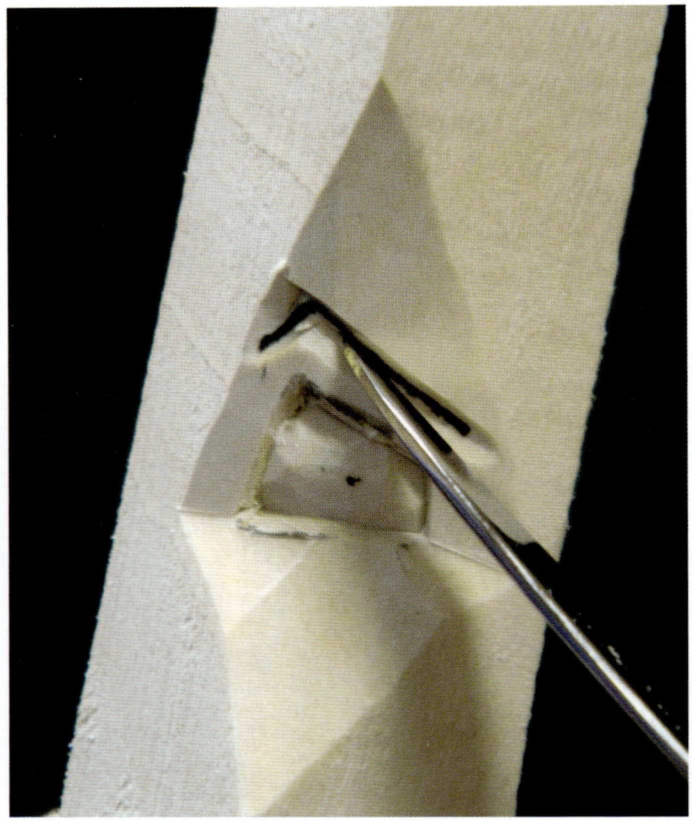

Stop cut along the line.

Now mark the crease of the eyelid and make a stop cut following the line.

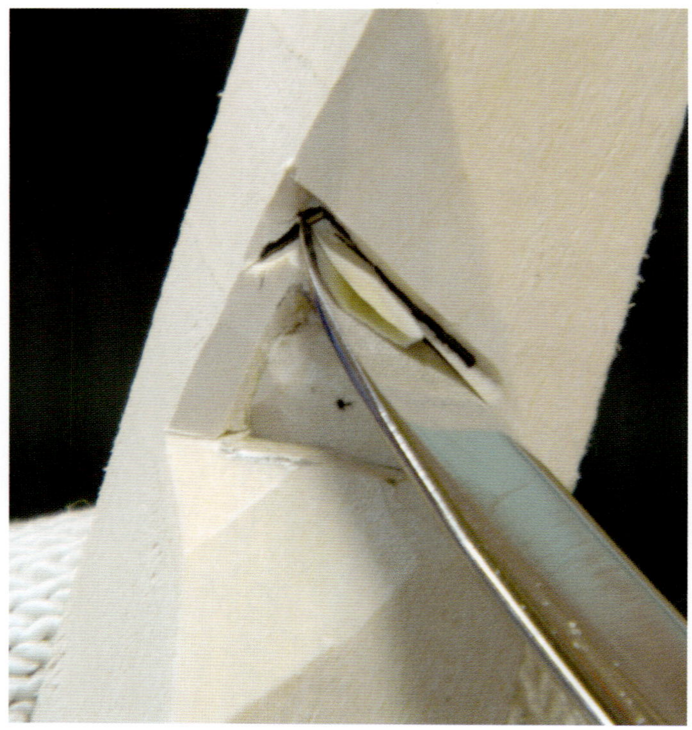

Make a thin cut back to the stop cut. This will thin out the material above the eyeball. These cuts should be made thin until you get the material removed down to the desired look. Pay close attention when making these cuts so that you do not break the eyelid and expose the top of the eyeball.

The thinning of the eyelid is now complete. Notice the cuts were made only towards the stop cut and no place else.

The eye is complete and the pupil is marked so you can see the direction that the eye is looking. When creating the eye, try different variations of the trapezoid shape, but keep in mind the widest point of the trapezoid is where the eye will be looking.

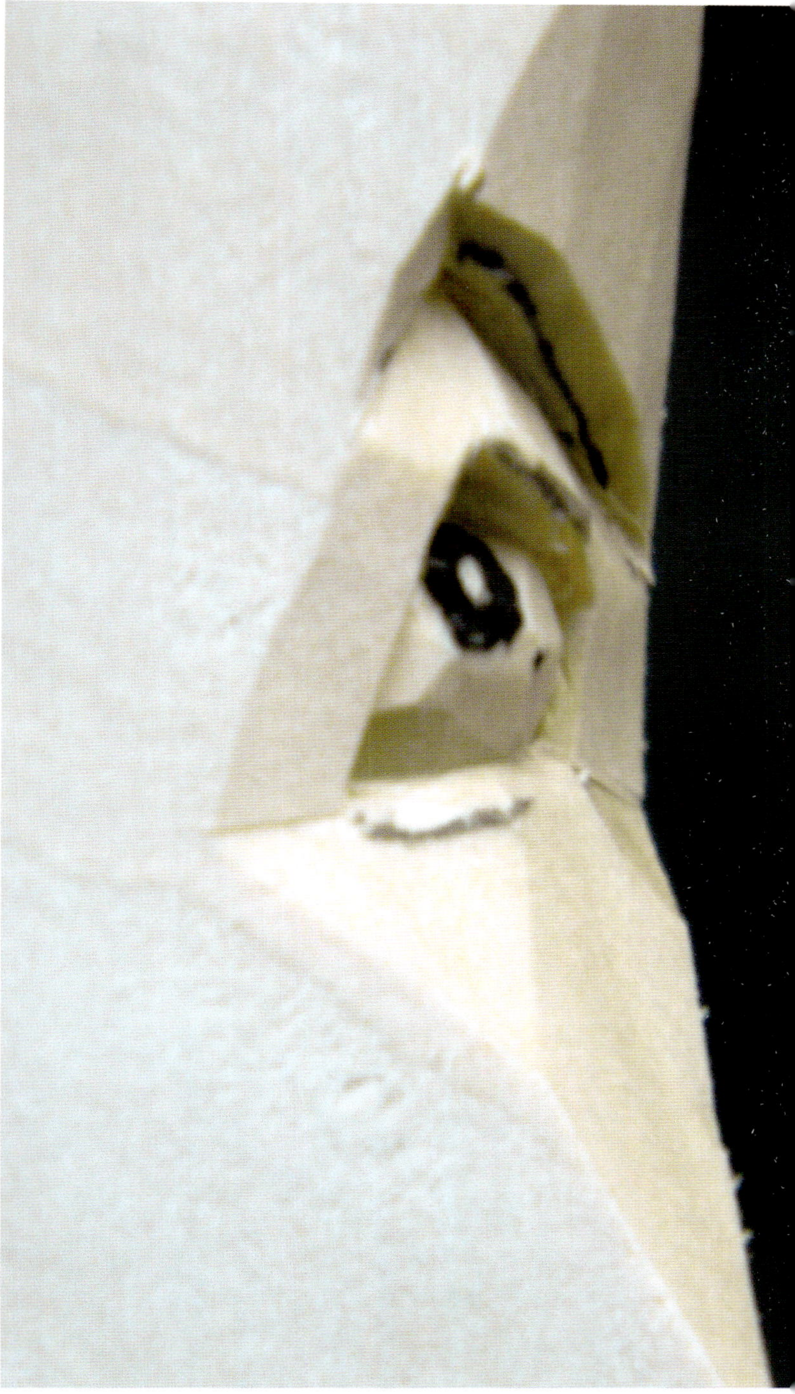

Here we have the completed eye from the side. This shows how deep we cut above the eye and the shape of the eyelid.

Chapter 3

Carving the Book Bookmark

Our first project is one that I came up with for a friend of mine. She needed something for a family member that was a book enthusiast and wanted something they did not have, so I came up with this carving for her.

The wood used for this project is flat stock basswood and will measure 3/8" thick, 1-1/4" wide, and 3" long. The direction of the grain should be running from left to right for this piece.

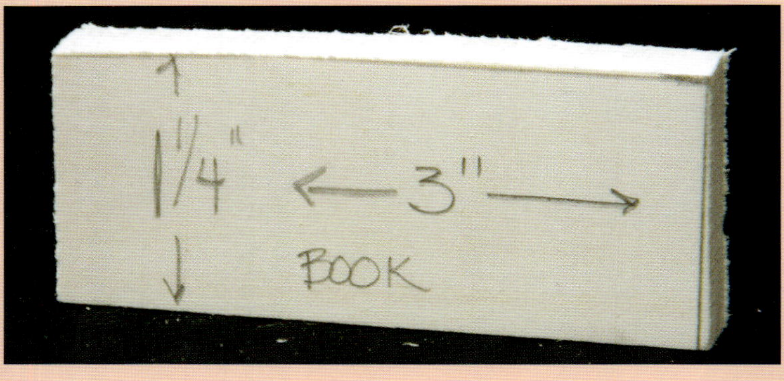

The blank for this project is 3/8" thick, 1-1/4" wide, and 3" long. The grain is running left to right in this piece.

Mark the middle of the block for the center of the book. The arrows shown are the directions we will be cutting back towards the center.

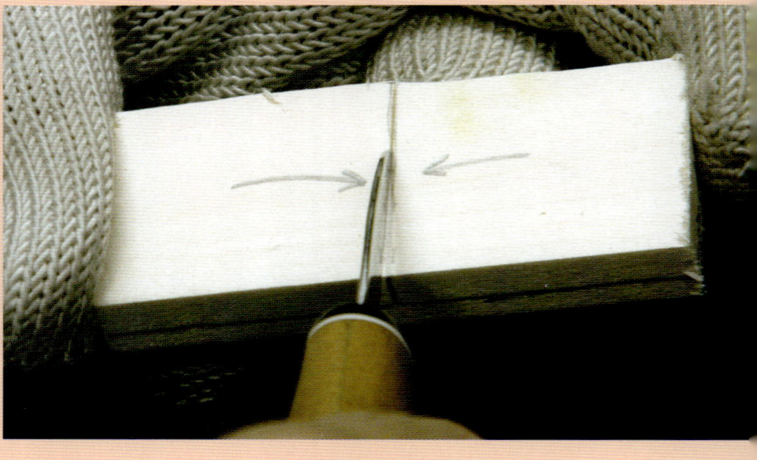

Make a stop cut along the line marked about an 1/8" deep. This cut can be made deeper to give the center pages of the book a more arched look.

Cut back towards the stop cut previously made on the end of the line.

Now cut the other side towards the stop cut. This will remove the piece of wood and a small v cut is created.

Make the same two cuts on the opposite side. Your blank should now look like this.

Making a pear cut, cut towards the center stop cut. Do this for both sides — the cuts should be the same width as the end cuts previously made.

Make a pear cut on the ends of the blank. This will give you approximately a 45-degree angle across the end. Repeat this on the other end.

Your cut should look like this. Next we will round the corners.

Make a push cut to clip the corners of the end. Do this for all four corners.

Start towards the middle and make a push cut towards the end rounding off the edge. Pay close attention to the grain of the wood. Do not dig into the wood too far.

One end complete.

We are now repeating the same cuts as the other end to round the book off.

Using a small v-tool, make your cut along the line marked around the bottom of the book.

One side completed with making the cut with the v-tool. Continue this cut all the way around the blank.

End of book cut with v-tool.

Now round off the ends of the book in the direction shown by the arrow.

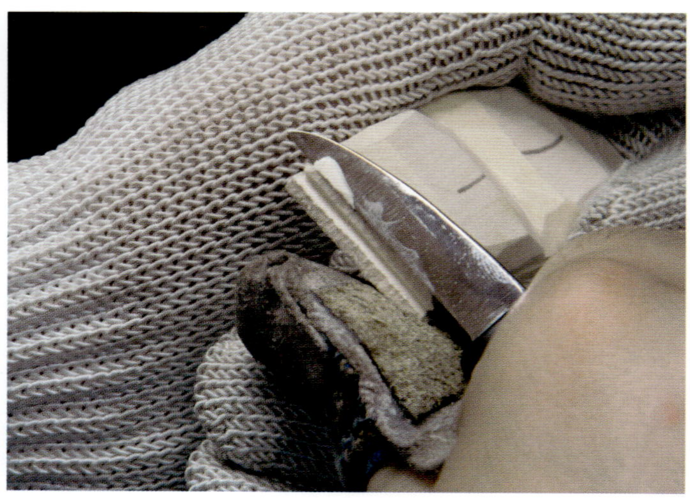

Make a pear cut towards the end of the book in the direction of the arrow rounding off the end.

One end completed. Repeat the same steps for the other end.

Using the v-tool wing, cut along the edge of the book in the direction marked by the arrow. By using just the wing of the tool, you will take away the hard "v" shape line that was created by using the bottom of the v-tool. Make this cut for the top and bottom of the book.

Your carving should look like this after using the wing of the tool on the top and bottom.

With the v-tool make some cuts on the top and bottom of the blank to create your pages.

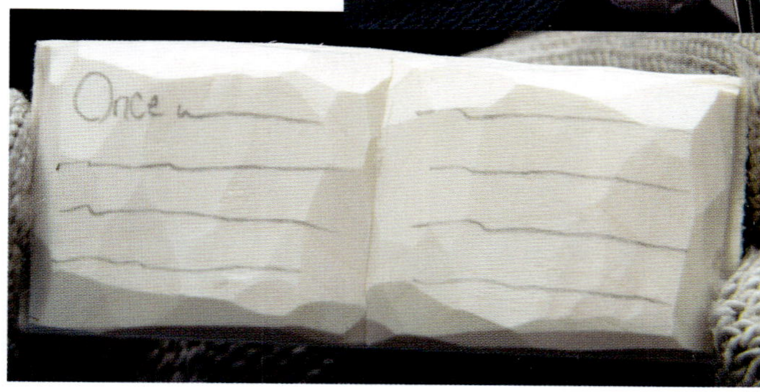

Draw some lines on the front pages of the book to look like writing. You can use a permanent marker or wood burner to create the lines.

The completed book bookmark; now we will carve the book place marker.

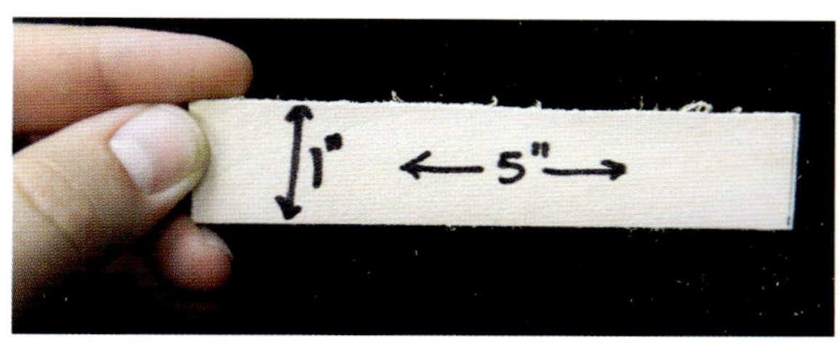

The book place marker is 1" x 5" x 3/8" piece of basswood. The grain in this piece runs left to right.

The beginning thickness of the place marker.

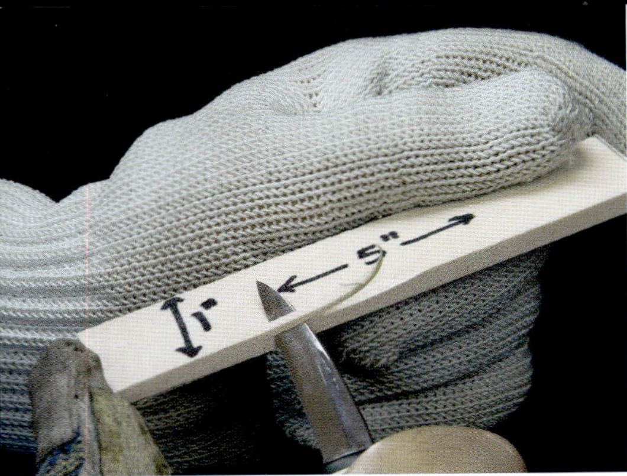

Start by making a pear cut along the edge of the blank. You will be rounding off both sides of this piece the same amount.

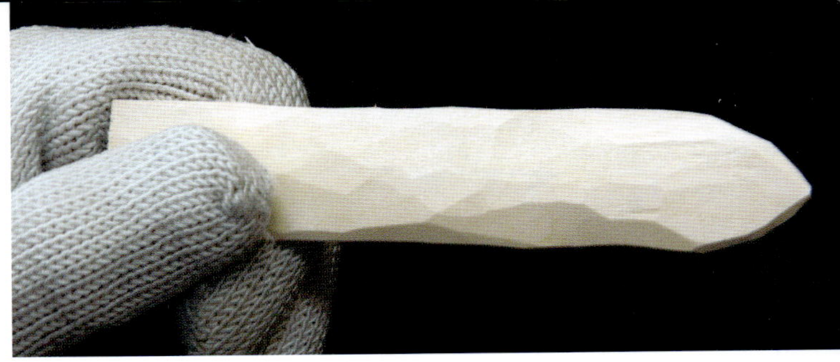

Our completed place marker. Notice the square end — this will be attached to the bookmark.

One end of the place marker needs to be tapered down to the thickness shown, which is just under an 1/8". This end will be used to mark the pages of a book.

With the place marker on the back side of the bookmark, line it up in the middle of the bookmark and mark the outer shape of the place marker with a pencil.

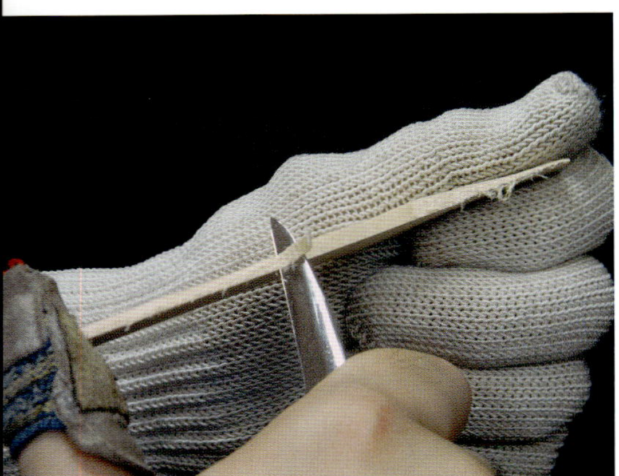

Continue to work the piece down to a thickness that you like. Keep in mind that this will need to fit into a book without being too thick.

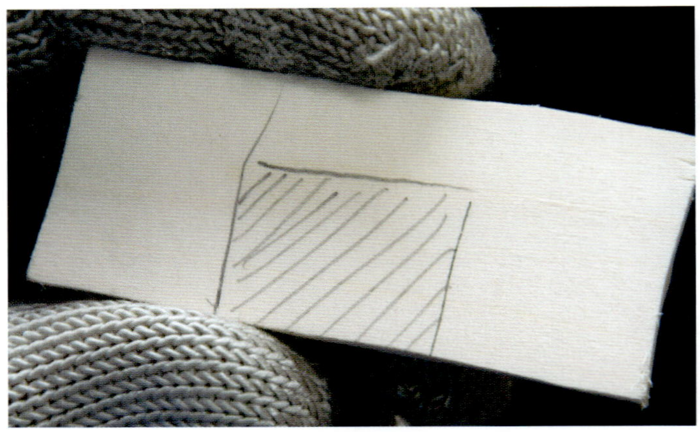

The area shaded will now be removed to receive the place marker.

Now taper the thin end of the place marker so that it is not perfectly square. You can make this completely round or just clip off the corners. I have marked the shaded areas for this one to be removed.

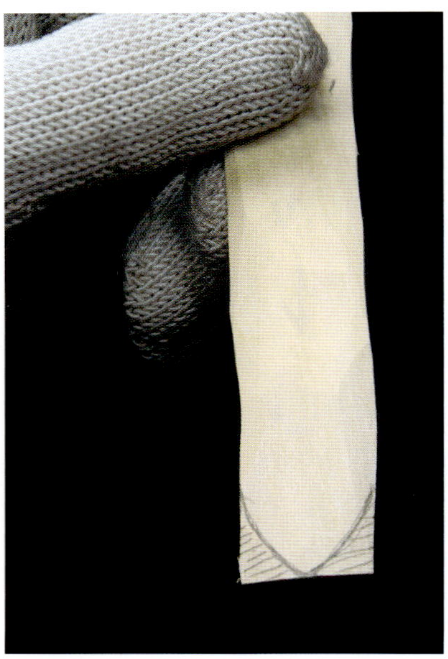

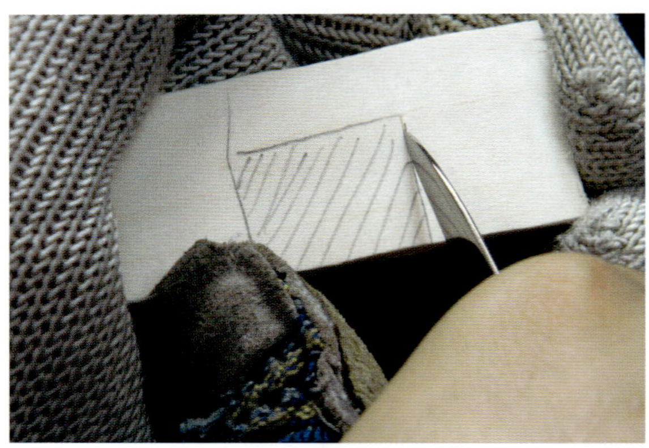

Start by making a stop cut along the lines marked on all three sides.

Make a push cut back towards the stop cut to remove the material.

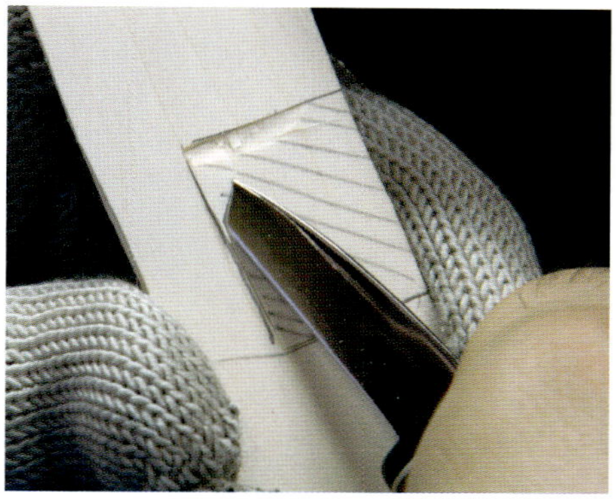

Cutting back towards the top line removing the corner.

Continue these cuts until you get enough material removed so that the place marker sits flush with the back of the bookmark.

This is what it should look like when done.

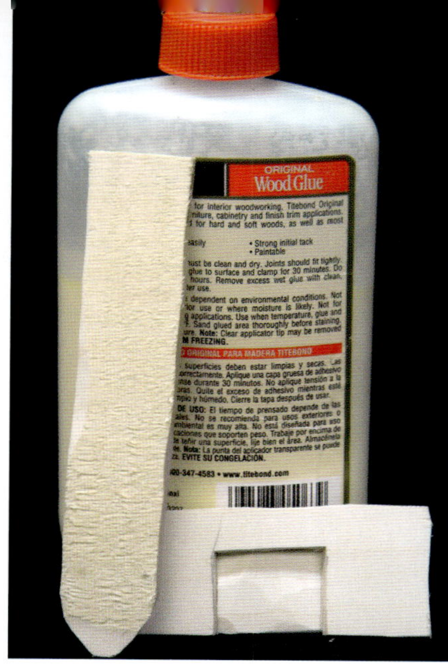

Next, glue the two pieces together using some wood glue. You can use super glue in place of the wood glue if you prefer.

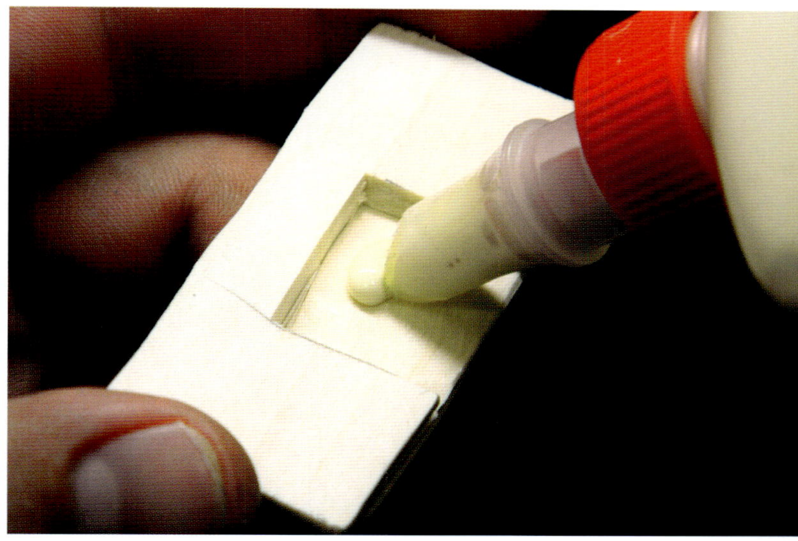

Add some glue to the cavity of the bookmark. Add just enough to get good coverage and not push the glue out the sides when you add the place marker.

Clamp the piece and let it dry. We will paint the piece in Chapter 4.

Chapter 4

Painting the Book Bookmark

Now that we are ready to paint the book bookmark, there are a few things we need to get prepared before we can actually paint. You will need a small and medium size paint brush, a container of water to wash your brushes in, a small pump spray bottle or container of water big enough to wet your carving, olive green acrylic paint and vanilla acrylic paint, and a paint tray or piece of glass to mix your paints. I prefer a piece of glass to mix my paints on, so I can control how thin or thick my colors are.

When thinning your paints down to paint the bookmark, you will add a drop or two of paint to the palette and then add three or four drops of water. Once you have mixed the two together, look for a thin consistency and uniform color. I do not paint straight from the bottle as this does not let the wood show through the paint. If you do get the colors too thick, simply add water to the carving and the colors will fade to the opacity you were looking for. If you apply the color to the carving and it seems too light, just add one drop of paint to your mixture until you get the desired consistency. Painting takes time to learn and can ruin a carving if not done with some care, so just take your time when painting the pieces.

The antique solution we will use after we have painted and dried the bookmark is a 50-50 mixture of boiled linseed oil and mineral spirits with half-a-tube of burnt umber oil based paint to add the darkness we are looking for to make it look older. I just mix these three items in a metal paint can and store it in a cool, dry place. When you are working with this solution, do not discard your rags or paper towels in the trash after you have wiped off the excess solution from your carving. The boiled linseed oil and mineral spirits can combust and possibly start a fire. To prevent this from happening, simply wet the paper towel before discarding it and let your cloth towel air-dry in the open.

This is the completed bookmark that I have wood-burned the lines on to show the appearance of text.

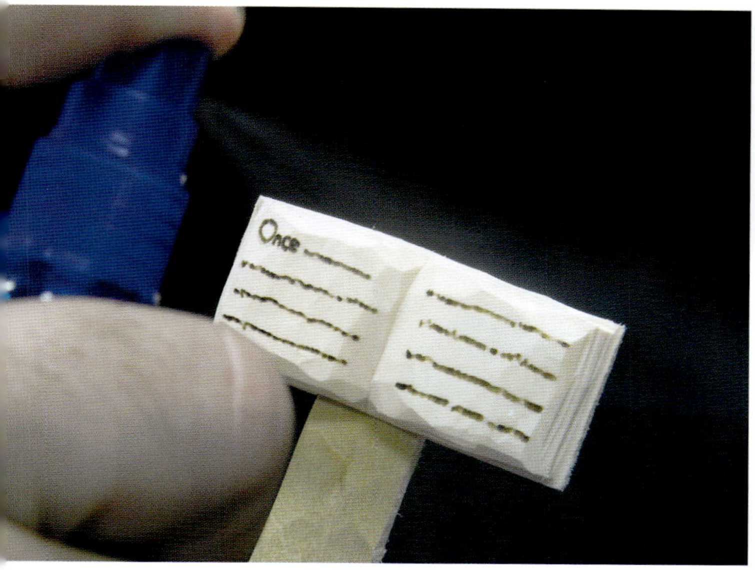

Start by spraying the piece with water.

With the Olive Green color, paint the ends of the book, but be careful not to paint the pages or edges of the book.

Continue along the bottom of the book.

Now onto the other side: Paint the Olive Green all the way around the book.

Turn the piece over and paint the back with the same color. Do not paint the place marker as we want it to be a natural color.

Make sure when painting the place marker to get a nice even color on the back and edges. You may apply two thin coats to make sure you get all of it painted.

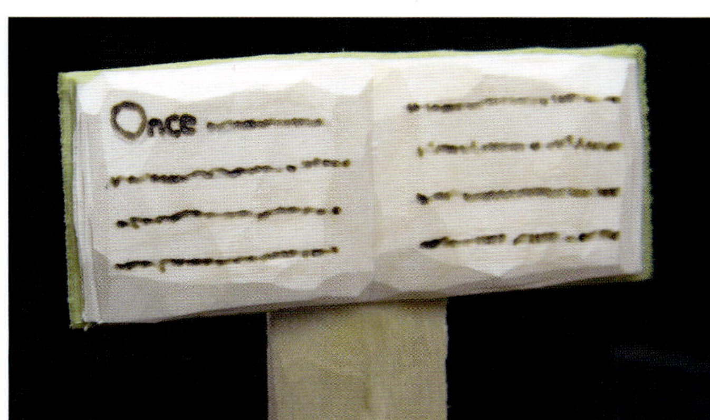

Now that the back and edges are painted, begin painting the pages of the book.

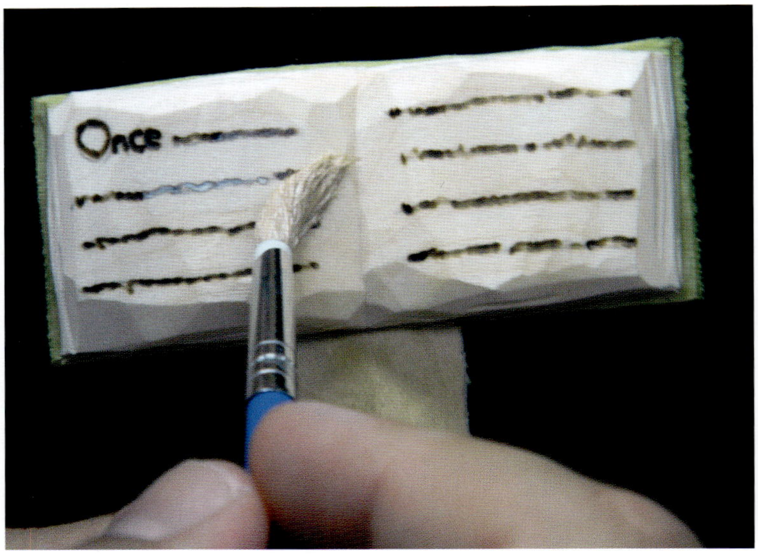

With the Vanilla color, start applying paint to the pages of the book.

You can see that the Vanilla color is very light against the basswood. Make sure you get even coverage over all the pages. Once the piece is antiqued, the color will be more defined.

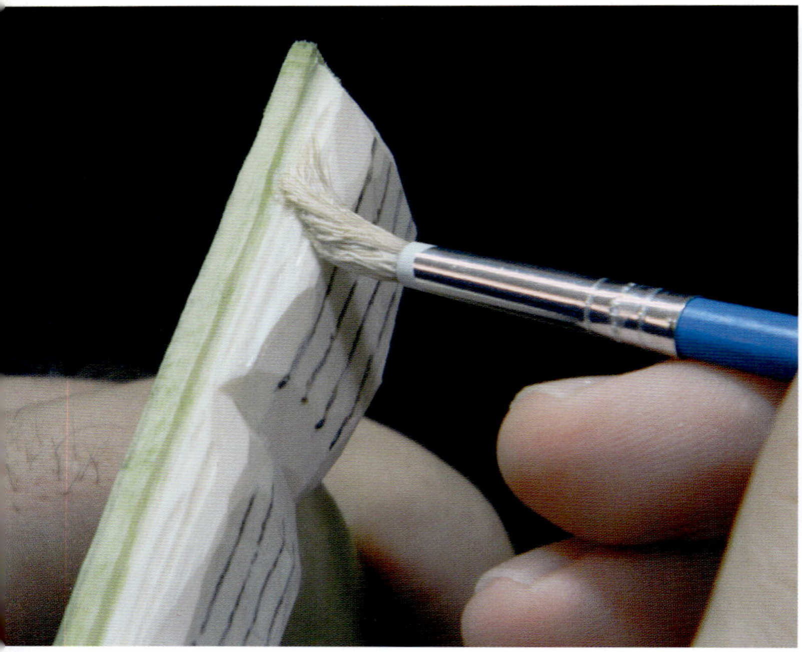

Paint the edges of the pages all the way around the book.

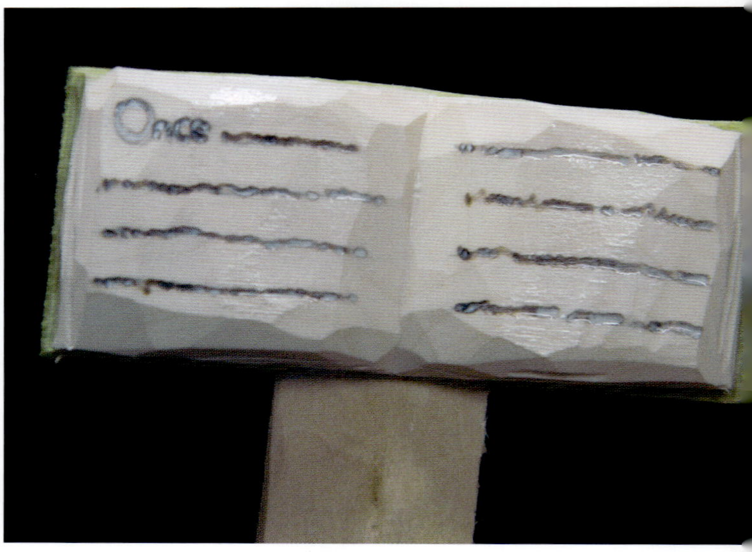

Your book should be now completely painted. After it is dry, we will antique the piece.

Dip the piece in the antique solution we have mixed up.

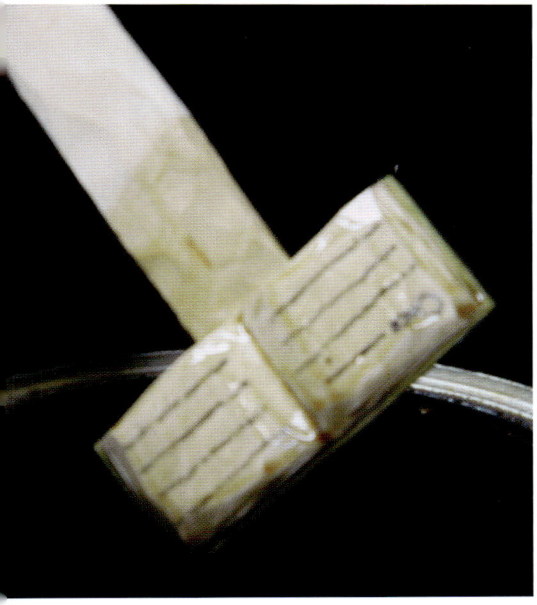

Half of the book dipped in the solution.

Wipe off the extra solution.

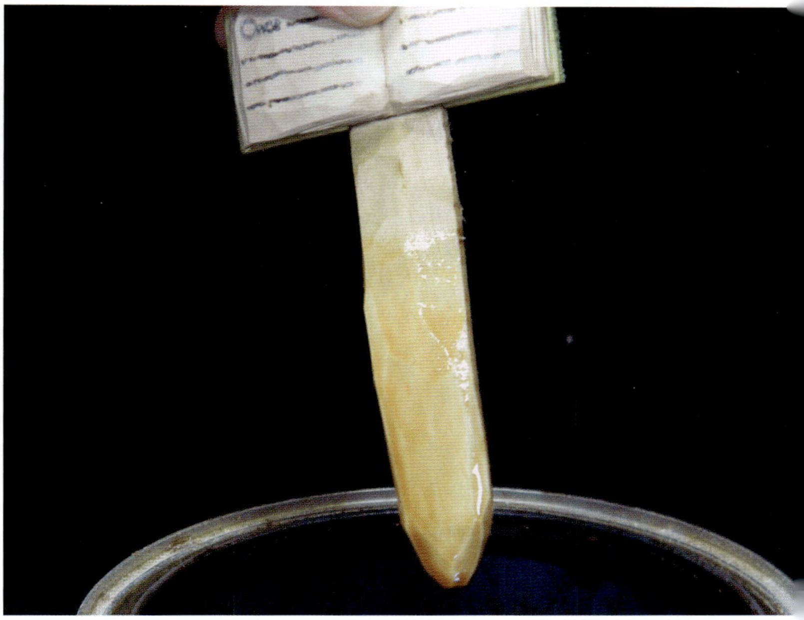

Dip the other half of the bookmark, wipe off the extra solution, and let the piece dry for 24 hours.

There you have it: A nice hand-carved book bookmark.

Chapter 5

Carving the Santa Bookmark

This Santa pattern for the bookmark actually started out as my Christmas ornament from a few years ago. I have taken that pattern and simply added the book page marker to make something special for the holidays.

The block of basswood is 1-1/2" thick by 1-1/2" wide by 2-3/4" long. We will cut it from a 12" long piece of basswood. We will be cutting this block on the band saw on its edge and, when completed, we will have two triangular shaped blocks that we can carve.

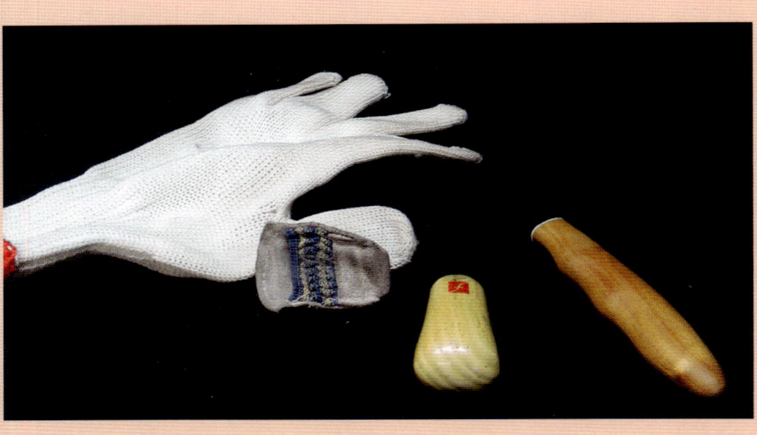

The tools for the Santa bookmark is a knife, small v-tool, safety glove, and thumb guard.

Line up the block on the line and slowly start cutting the block to the length marked.

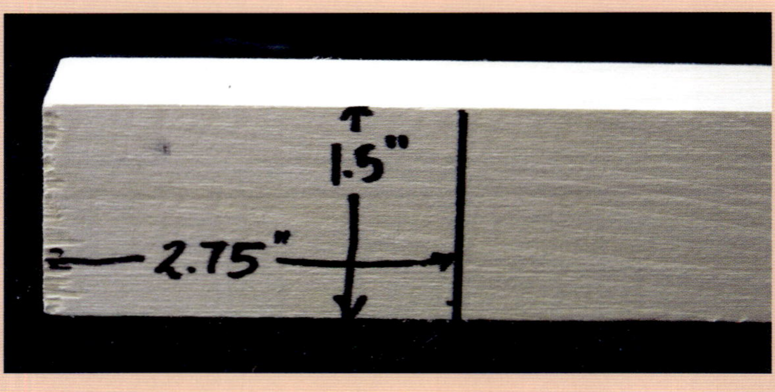

The block should measure 1-1/2" x 1-1/2" x 2-3/4" and will be cut diagonally.

Make a line diagonally across the block. I will cut this on the band saw along the diagonal line. If you do not have a band saw, you can use a miter box saw to make the cut.

We are half way to the desired length. Guide the block with both hands so that it does not lean to one side. Once you reach the length, pull the piece out and cut it free of the remaining block.

Side view showing our cut block on the diagonal and cut free from the rest of the block of wood.

Here is our Santa block ready to carve.

I used the other half of the block we just cut and marked out the bridge of the nose about 1" from the top.

Make a stop cut on the line we made about an 1/8" deep.

Make a push cut back up towards the stop cut to connect the two pieces.

Top of the bridge of the nose made.

Cut down towards the stop cut to make our v -shape. This makes the start of the forehead above the bridge of the nose.

Here are our completed cuts. The upper cut can be a lot longer than the bottom cut as this material will be rounded off later.

Next, remove the material towards the middle of the existing v-cut in the directions indicated by the arrows.

Starting at the bottom cut, take the knife and make your cut towards the middle.

From the top make the same cut towards the middle. This will release the piece of wood.

The two cuts completed and now the eye plane is established. Repeat this for the other side of the eye.

Both sides of the eye plane completed.

Next, mark the bottom of the nose about 2" from the top and approximately 3/8" on either side.

Make a stop cut on the line we made at 1/8" deep.

Next we will make a push cut back towards the stop cut. The direction is marked with the arrow.

The nose at the bottom was made wider the same way as we did on the top of the nose towards the eye plane. Do this for both sides.

Side view of the piece removed.

Now we will mark the flares of the nose as shown.

Front view of the top and bottom nose completed.

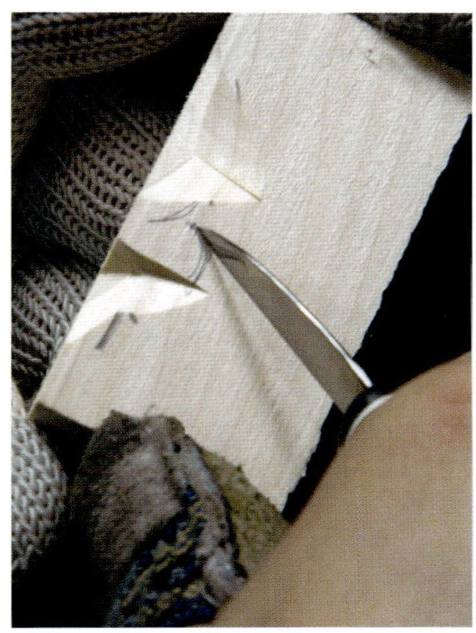

Make a stop cut along the lines marked.

Your block should look close to this one. If it doesn't, remove some more material to get the depth you would like.

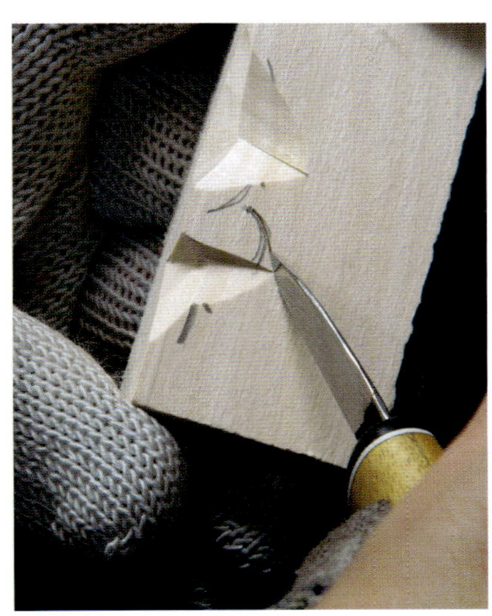

The stop cut will continue down the line. Notice how we varied off the line just a small amount and created a small triangle from our marked line to where the knife is located.

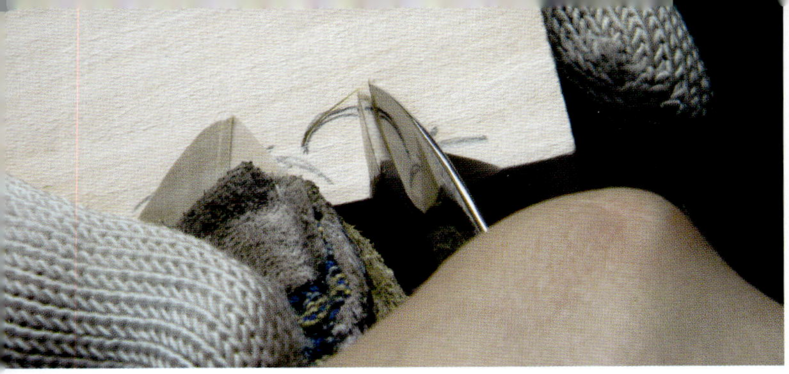

Now, from the bottom, make your cut up towards the flare of the nose and remove the small triangle with a stop cut on the line where we did not cut before.

Both stop cuts made and the cut up to the bottom of the nose. See how that triangle piece is now removed. Repeat this on the other side.

Repeated cuts on both sides now complete.

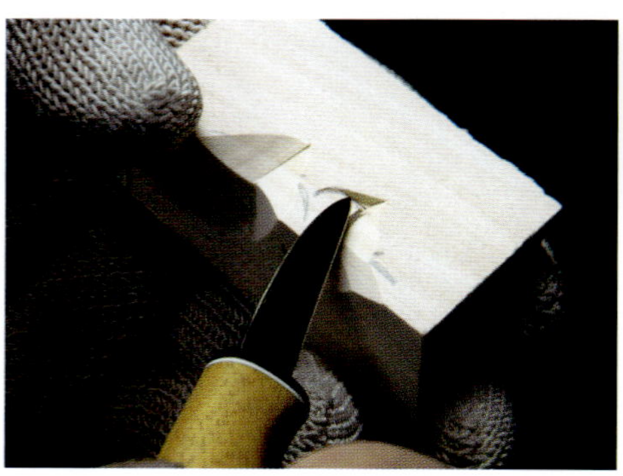

Now round off the corners of the nose so that there is no pointed edges.

Round off the bottom of the nose to take away that edge of the wood.

Cut towards the eye plane to round off the bridge of the nose.

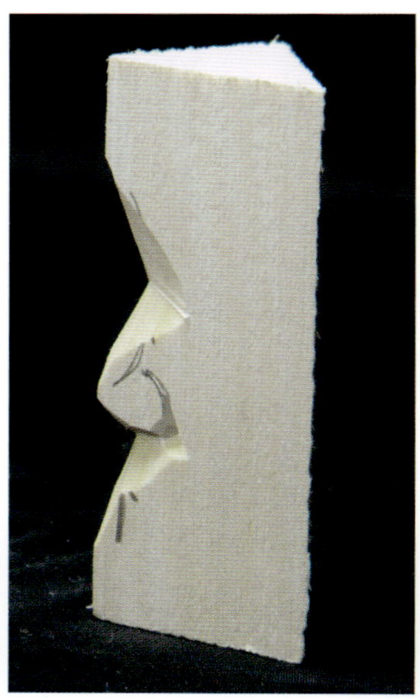

Side view after we rounded off the flares and bridge of the nose.

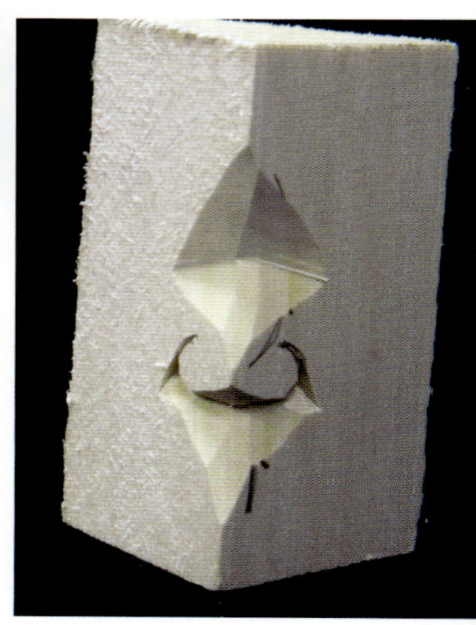

Your nose should look like this after completing those steps. If the cuts are not deep enough, repeat the steps to deepen them in the corners of the flares.

The arrows indicated are for thinning the bridge of the nose. The cut you will make is like a scooping motion and will need to be made a little at a time so that the knife does not dig into the wood.

Next, round off the bridge of the nose in small amounts.

The scooping cut being made towards the eye plane. Notice how the knife is fairly flat against the wood.

The arrow marked will be the direction of our next cut towards the bridge of the nose. Make the same scooping motion as the cut towards the eye plane.

One side done.

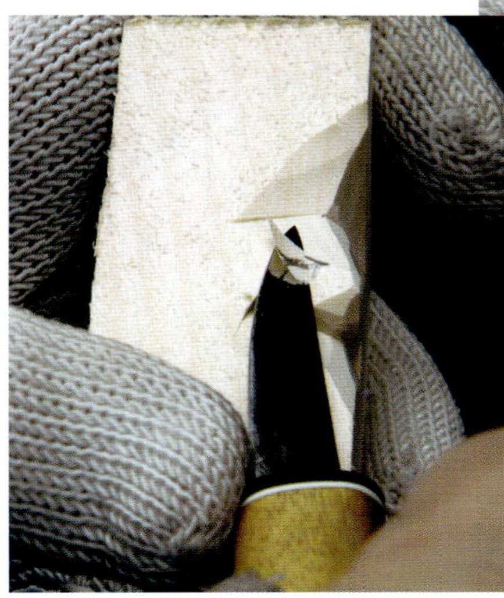

Easy thin cuts towards the bridge of the nose. Repeat this process on both sides.

With a small u-gouge, we will add nostrils. You can omit this step if you do not have a u-gouge. Add another nostril to the other side.

Remove the other side the same way towards the eye plane.

Completed nostril cuts.

Round the corners of the flares again to get the completed look.

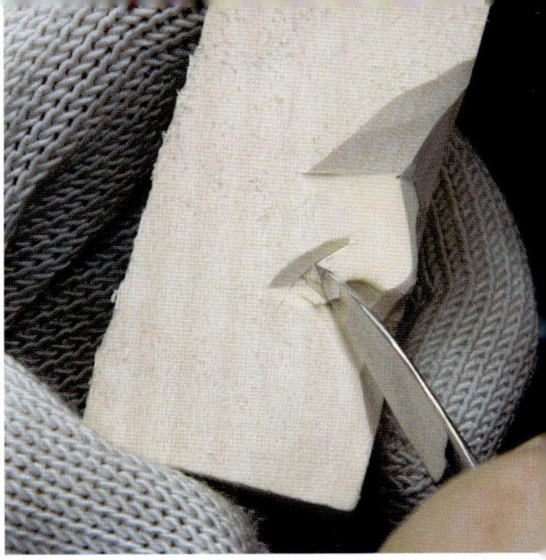

Now, make a stop cut along the previously cut areas so that we can round the sides of the flares of the nose.

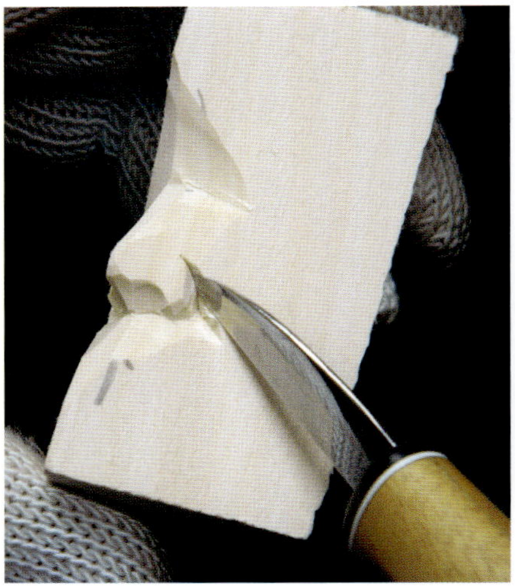

The nose is now complete.

Remove the material around the flares so that they can be rounded off.

The eyes have been marked and are trapezoid in shape. You can refer to Chapter 2 to have a better understanding when making the eye cuts.

Cut back towards the bottom to remove the material. These are the same cuts we made when cutting the flares.

In the corner of the marked eye, put the tip of the knife in and roll it towards the right side of the eye.

Rolling the knife tip towards the right. This cut takes practice so don't get discouraged. You can repeat this process to get the depth needed.

Corner one of the eye completed.

Small area removed. Now we are ready to start the eye.

Stop cut along the right side of the eye.

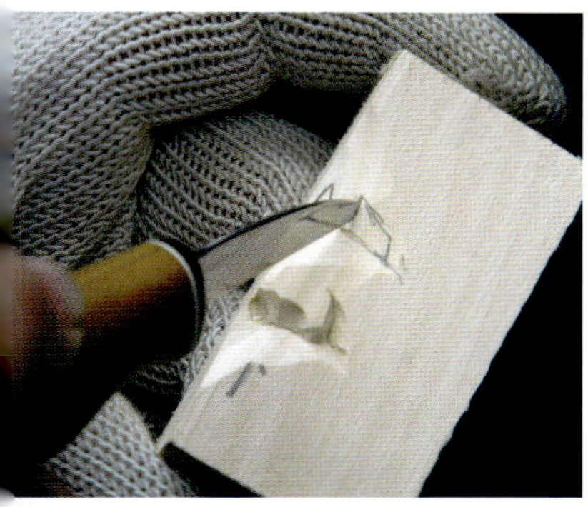

Make a stop cut in the first corner about an 1/8" deep.

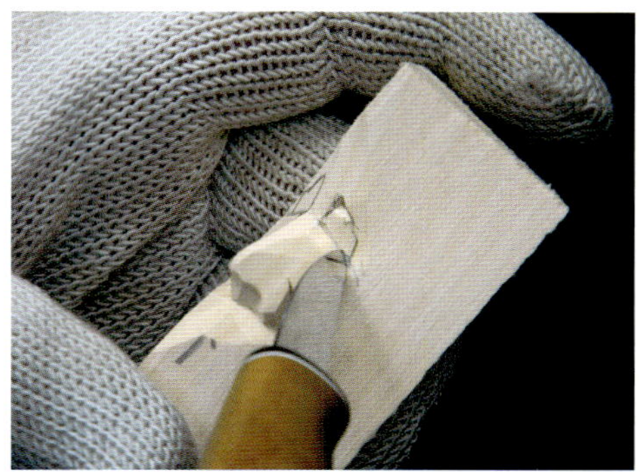

Stop cut along the bottom of the right side. Make a diagonal cut back towards the two cuts just like the corner one and remove the wood.

Stop cut the other side of the first corner the same depth as the other cut.

Two corners are now complete. Finish corner three and four the same way as one and two.

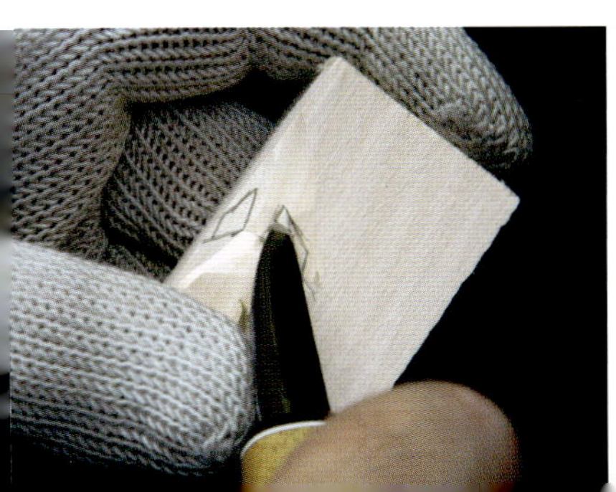

Make a push cut and remove the triangle piece of wood.

All four corners are now completed. Round off the eyeball to complete the eye.

Both eyes completed using the same cuts from the first eye.

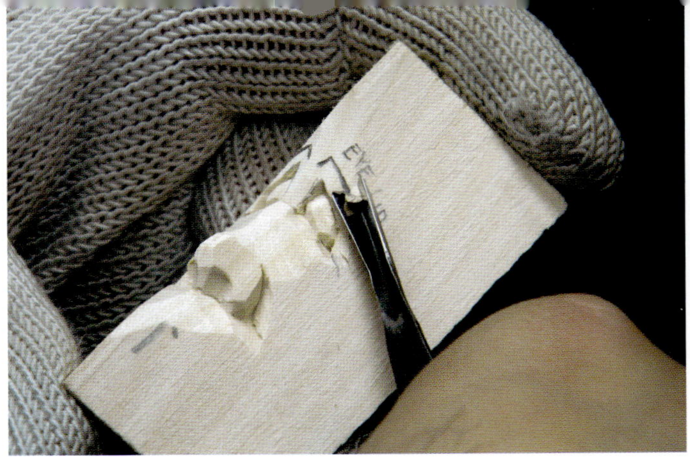

Make another cut with the v-tool along the top line towards the mark on the left.

The top eyelid is now marked about an 1/8" above the eye. The markings follow the shape of the trapezoidal eye we marked when laying out the eye.

Cut two done: The top of the eye lid is now set.

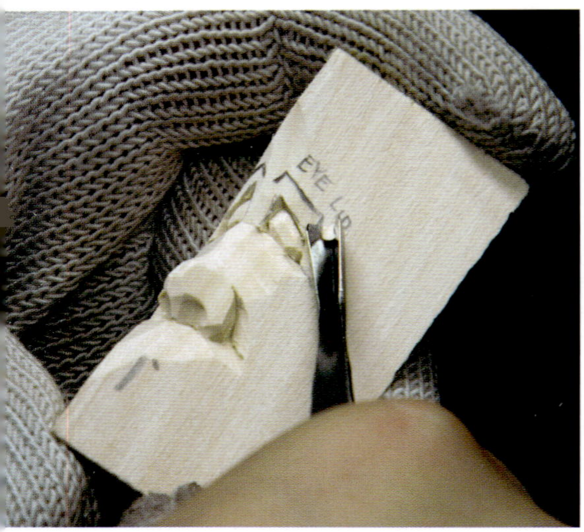

With the v-tool make the first cut on the line towards the line marked on the top.

The third cut is made with the v-tool towards the top cut. Repeat these three cuts for the other eyelid.

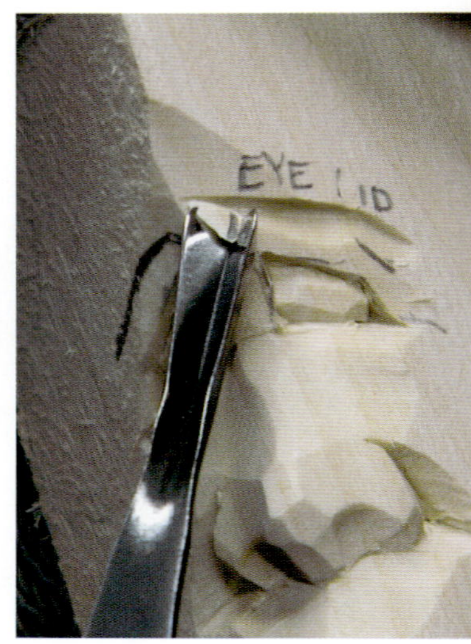

Cut completed: The right side of the eyelid is set.

Both eyelids are now completed — now we start shaping them.

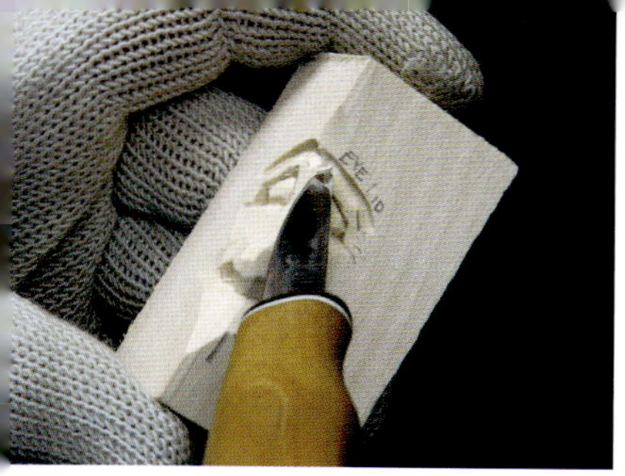

With your knife, clean up any pieces of wood remaining after making the v-cuts.

Both eyelids are completed and looking good.

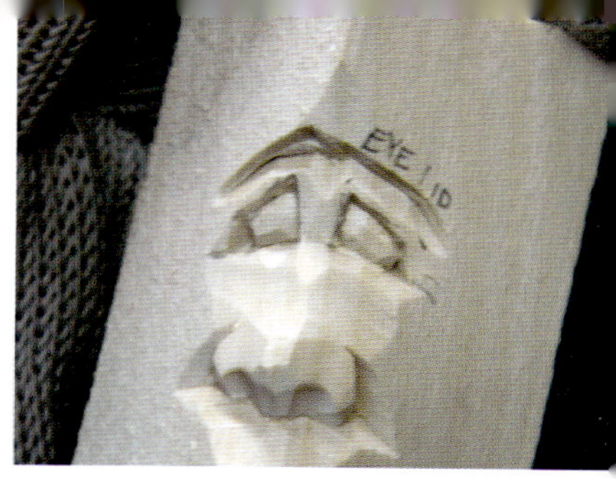

Make a stop cut along the middle of the v-cuts that we made on both sides of the eyelids.

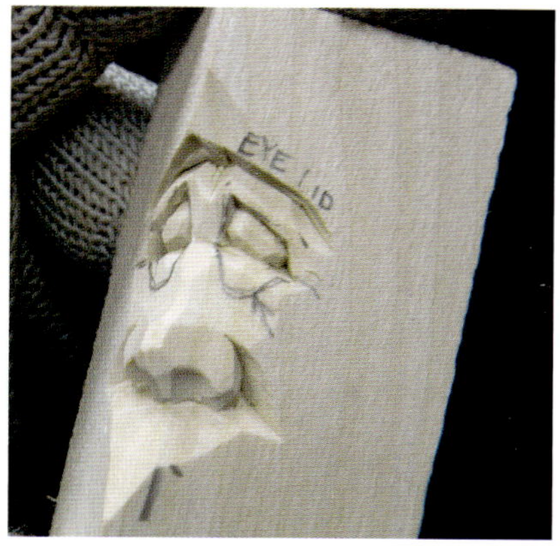

Now, mark the bottom eyelids or bags under the eyes.

Notice the stop cut line in the v-cut. Mark the direction of the next cut. This cut will thin the eyelids and give it a cleaner look.

Make a stop cut along the line we just marked.

Cut back to the stop cut along the bottom.

With the knife, make thin cuts towards the stop cut. Take a little off at a time to get the thickness you like. Be careful not to cut too deep and expose the eyeball.

Once the cut is completed, the piece of wood should pop out.

Now, cut from the side towards our stop cut and remove the wood.

The bottom eyelid is done. Repeat the cuts on the opposite side.

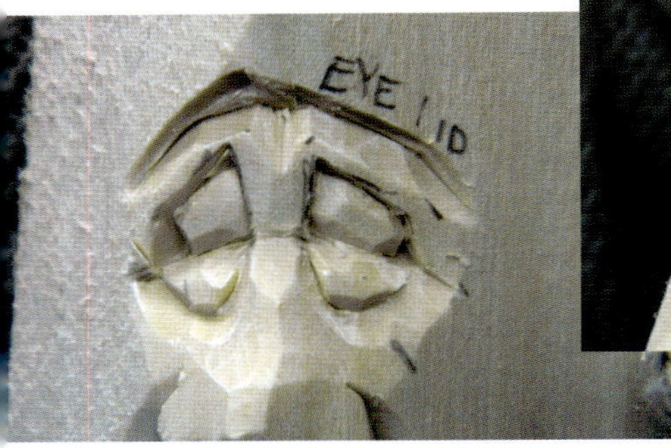

Both eyelids are done. The picture shows the edges rounded off to give a smooth appearance.

Now that the eyes and nose are done, mark the rest of the pattern on the block. You can mark the entire pattern before you start with any of the carving to help with proportions.

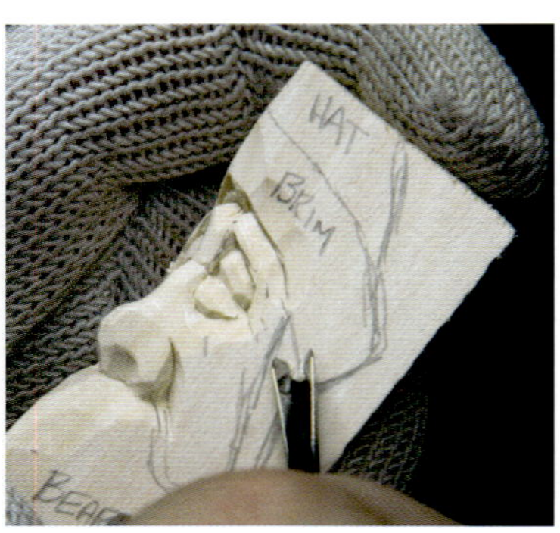

With your v-tool, follow the bottom line of the brim to the top of the eyelids and the end of the brim.

Same cut with the v-tool — along the line on the top of the brim separating the hat line.

Top, bottom, and side of the brim cut with the v-tool.

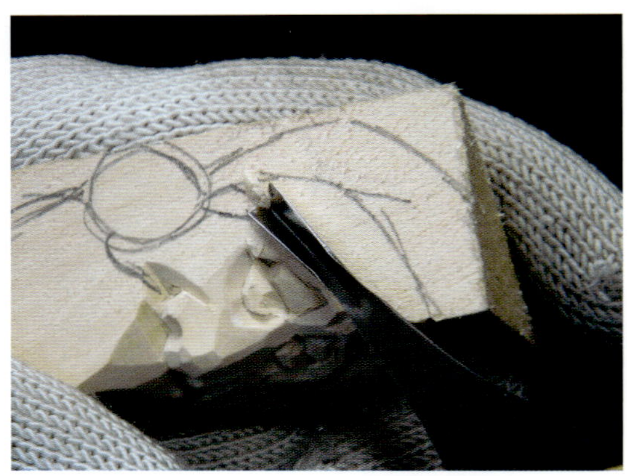

Repeat the top and bottom cuts of the brim on the other side. Cut only to the end of the lines marked.

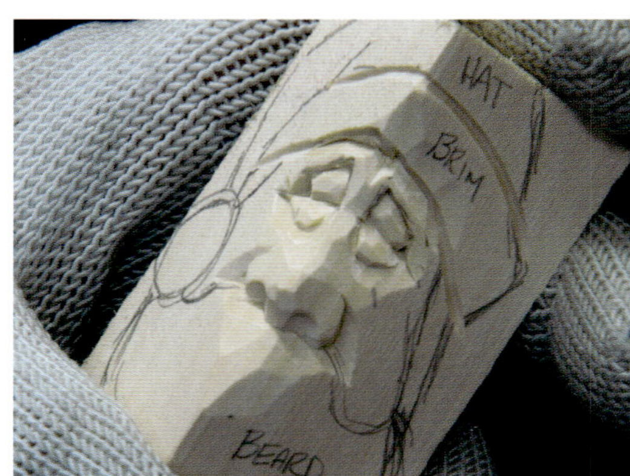

Top and bottom cuts completed.

Follow the line marked along the side of the hat up to the top.

Finish the cut and then cut the bottom of the cheek along the line marked.

Your cuts should look like this one. Notice that the v-cut goes from the flare of the nose all the way to the top of the brim.

Continue to cut through the brim area. This will separate the brim from the side.

Finish the cut at the end of the line marked.

Now go to the other side and remove the line from the flare of the nose to the ball of the hat.

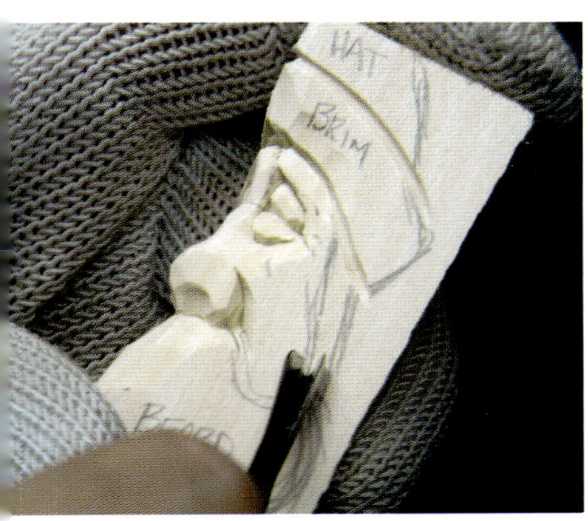

With the v-tool, cut along the beard line up towards the brim of the hat starting at the bottom of the cheek.

With the v-tool, outline the ball of the hat, just like the picture.

Make a pear cut down to the stop cut.

Mark the area around the cuts we just made and the area on the mustache that will be removed.

Start by making a pear cut and remove the material.

Make a stop cut from the outside block to the top of the brim.

Make a stop cut from the outside of the block to the bottom of the brim.

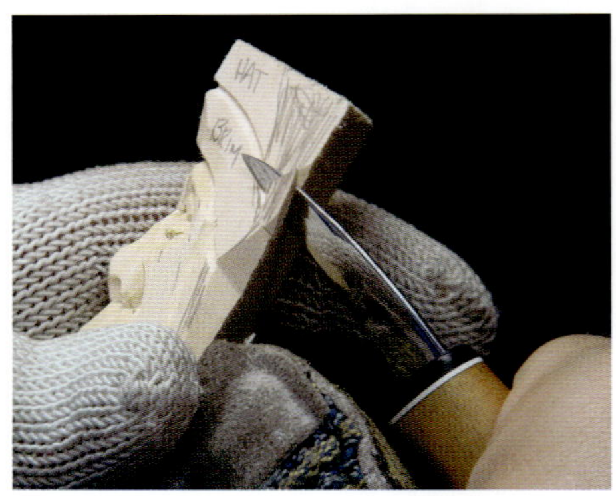

Make a pear cut down to the stop cut and continue removing the shaded area.

The right side of the material has been removed; continue removing the wood on the other side until it's all removed.

Push cut up to the stop cut and remove the wood.

Both sides of the Santa removed.

Both sides of the brim completed.

Make a stop cut at the top of the brim in the middle and then down both sides of the brim.

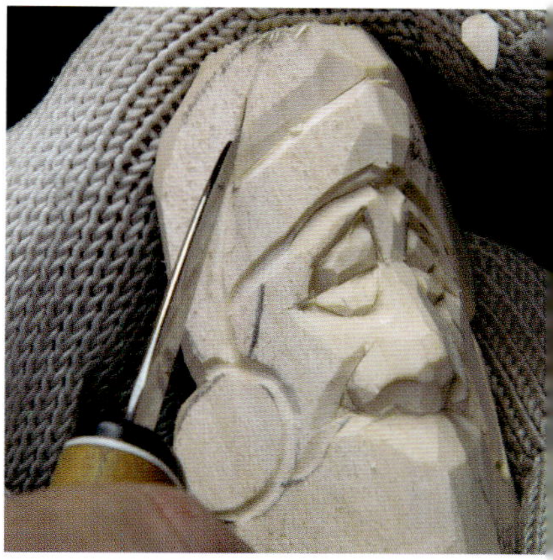

Stop cut the crease of the hat from the top down towards the ball.

Cutting towards the stop cut, remove the wood a little at a time until the brim is rounded off.

Stopping at the ball with our stop cut.

Continue down the brim cutting towards the stop cut.

The arrows marked will be our next cut towards the stop cut and bring the brim under the side of the hat.

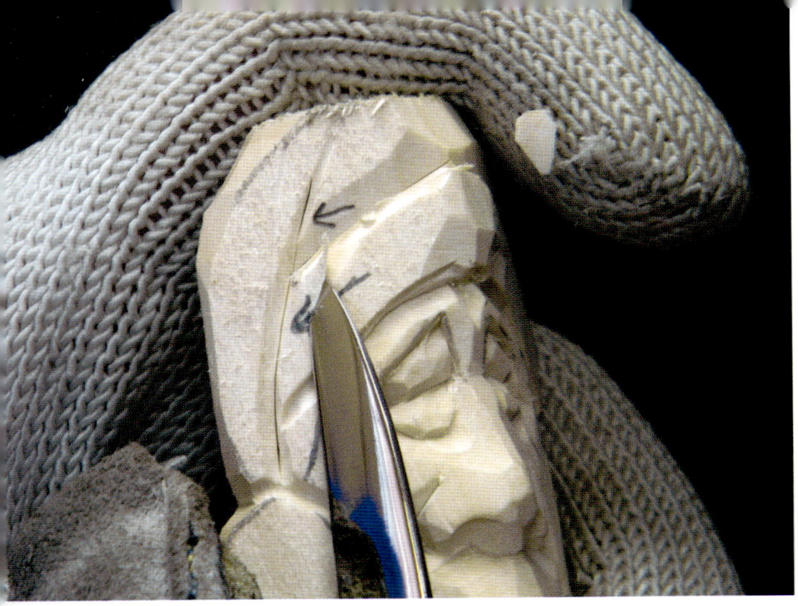

Thin cuts are needed here to shape the brim.

Next, we will shape the side of the hat the same way we did the brim.

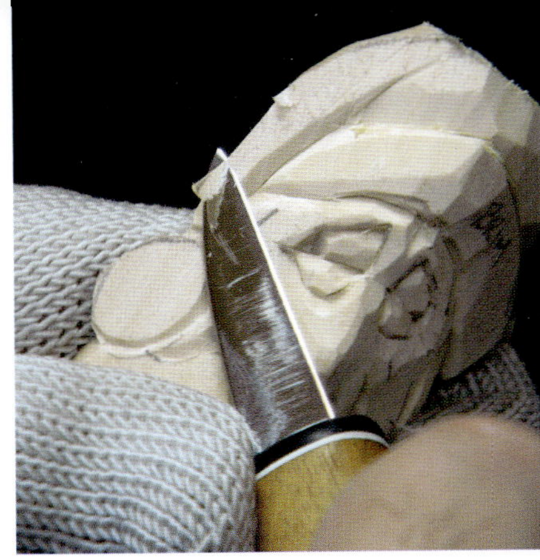

One side is done; now do the other side.

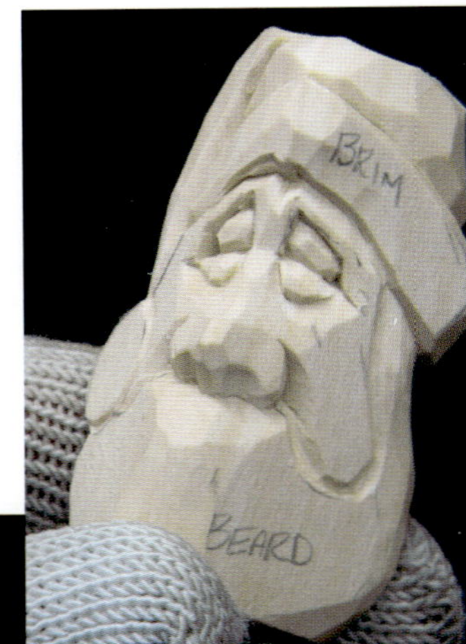

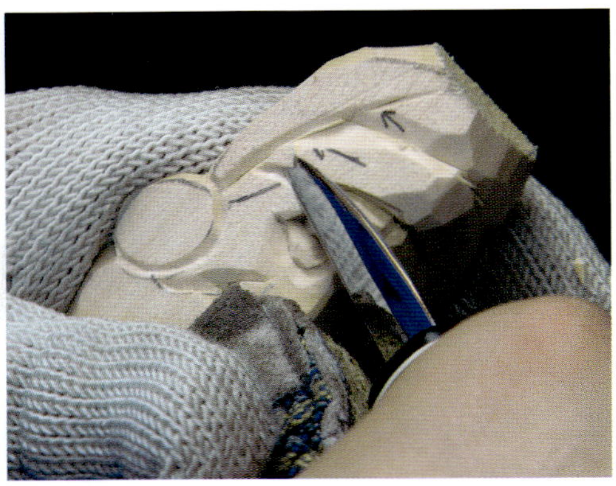

Making the same cuts along the side; rounding off the bottom of the brim.

Thin cuts to shape the other side of the brim.

Now, we are cutting back to the middle, shaping the brim of the hat.

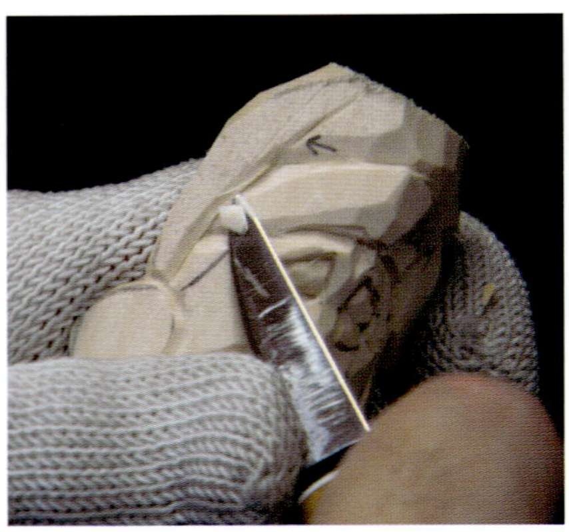

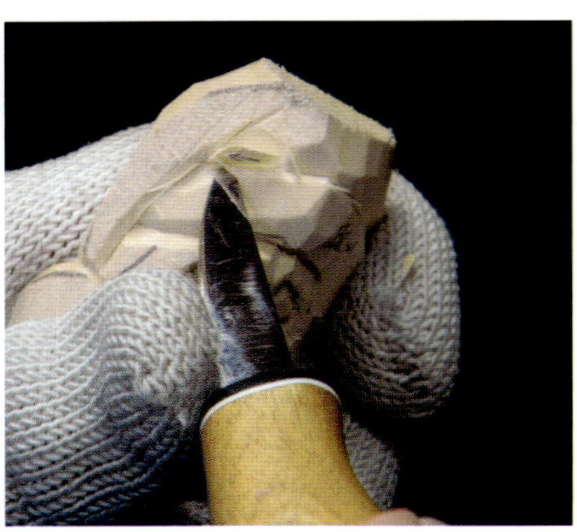

Shape the brim with thin cuts.

Make a stop cut along the right side of the face starting at the top.

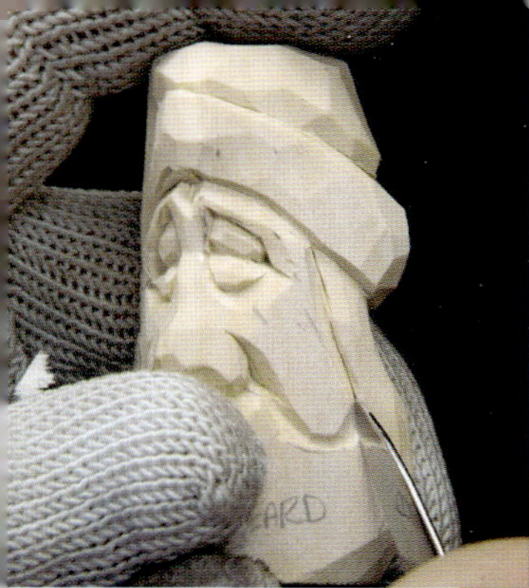

Continue the stop cut down the side towards the bottom of the cheek.

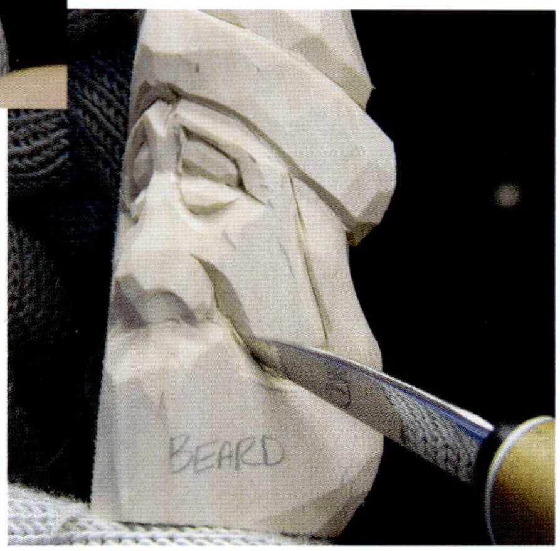

From the corner of the nose bring the stop cut towards the previous stop cut at the bottom of the cheek.

Next, we will mark the direction of our cuts to round off the cheek. These are the same thin cuts we did on the brim.

Cheeks and side of the face cut back towards our stop cut.

Make a stop cut on the opposite side of the face down to the ball on the hat.

Push cut back up towards the brim, removing the wood. This will create the side hairline and separate the cheeks.

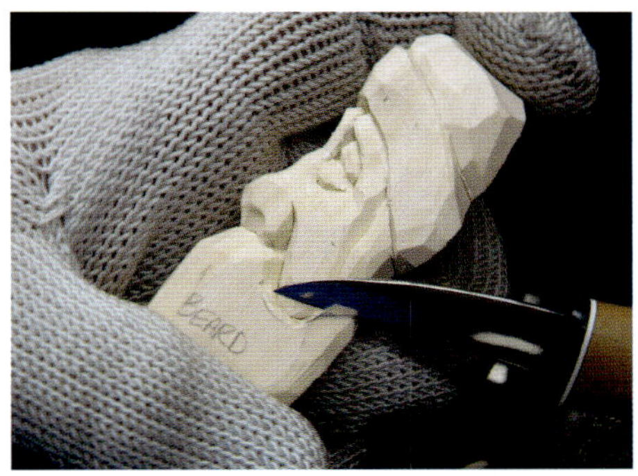

On the right side, make two cuts at the end of the mustache to make a v-shape.

Completed cuts at the end of the mustache.

Now, shape the mustache by making a push cut towards the nose.

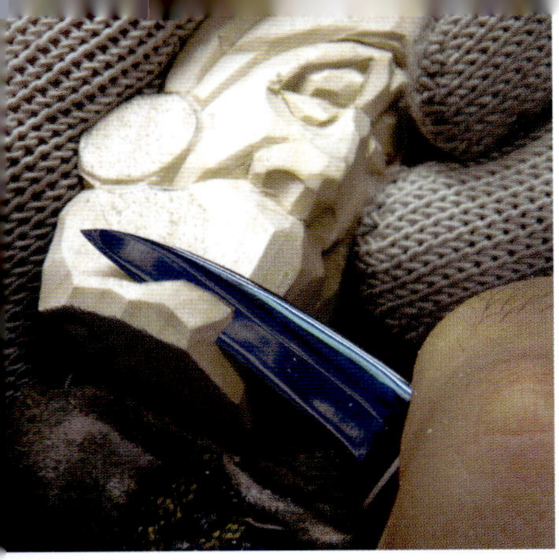

Make a pear cut and round off the bottom of the mustache.

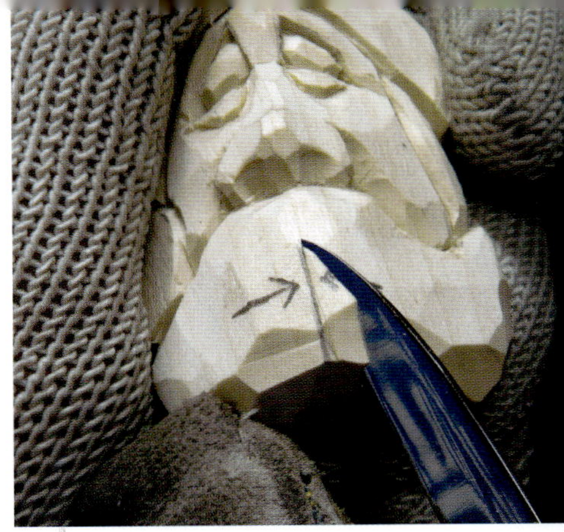

Along the arrows marked, cut back towards the stop cut.

One side of the mustache is complete. Make the same series of cuts for the other side.

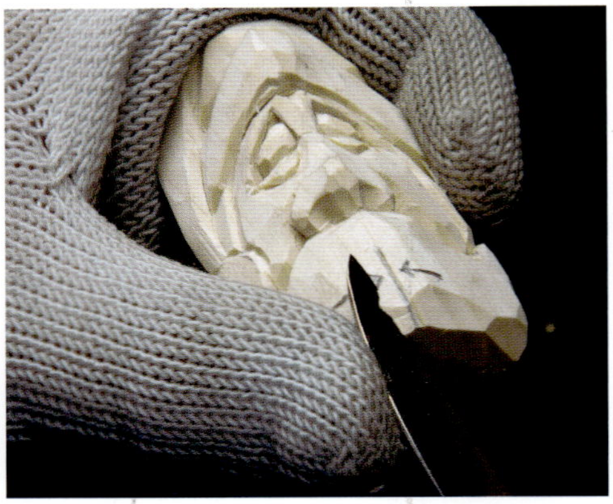

Repeat the process on the opposite side as shown.

In the center of the mustache, mark a line dividing the two sections of the mustache.

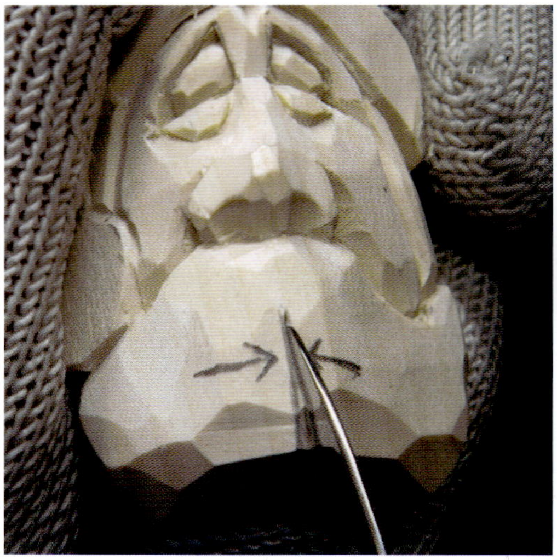

Make a stop cut fairly deep along the line.

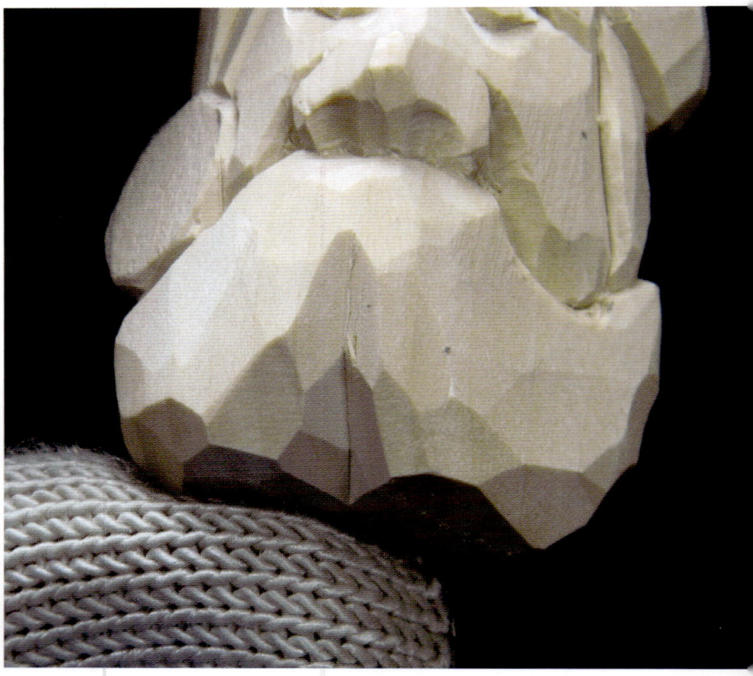

The middle piece is now removed separating the mustache.

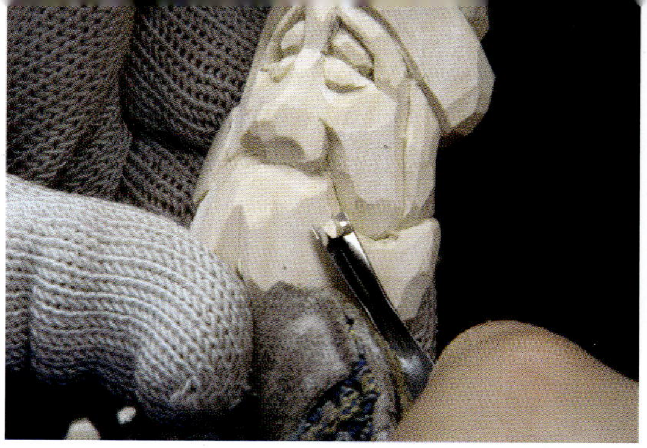

With the v-tool, make cuts along the curve of the mustache towards the bottom of the nose.

Both sides of the mustache are completed. Now, mark the ball to make the same v-cuts to define the texture on the ball.

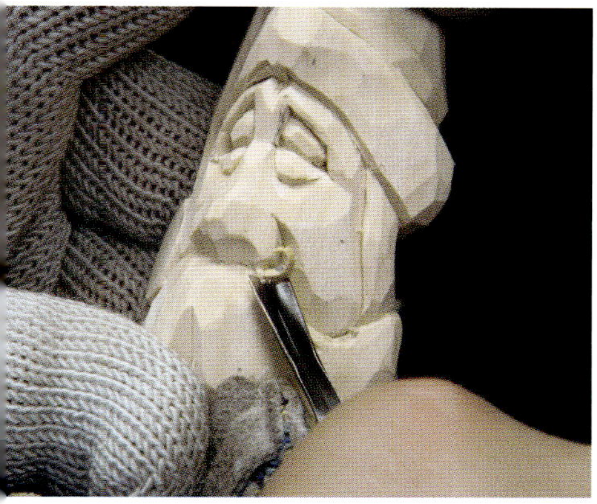

Stop just before the bottom of the nose.

Side view showing the mustache.

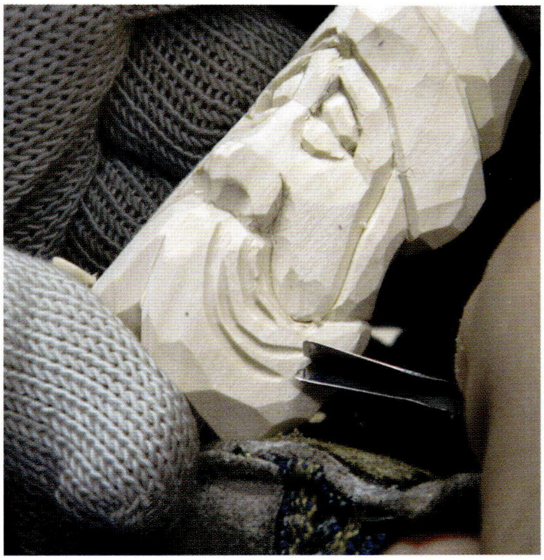

Keep making v-cuts along the curve until the mustache is well defined with hair.

With the v-tool, make a series of cuts starting from the center and cut out towards the mustache. When done, it should look something like this.

One side of the mustache is now complete. Continue this on the other side.

Here is the completed Santa. You can make a series of v-cuts along the side of the hat to add some character, thereby giving the piece the look of being wrinkled.

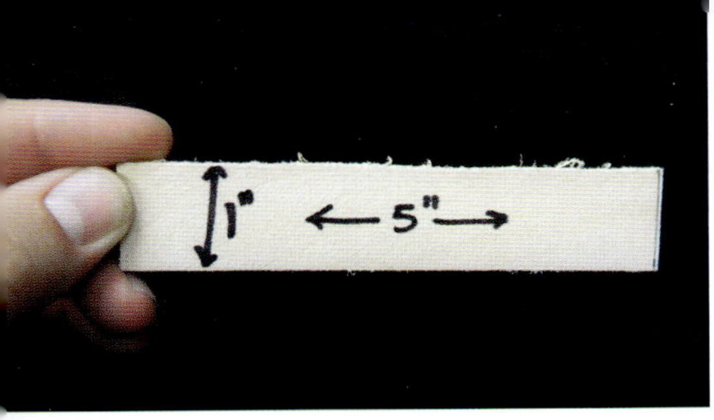

The book place marker is 1" x 5" x 3/8" piece of basswood. The grain in this piece runs left to right.

The beginning thickness of the place marker.

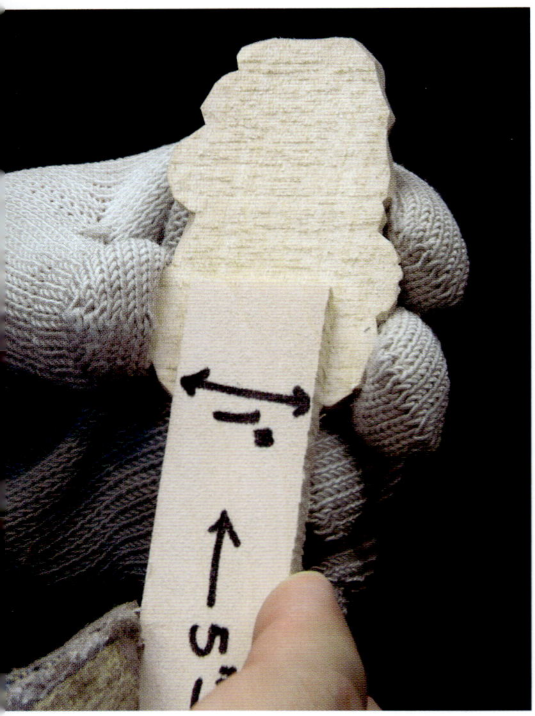

We mark the back side of the Santa with our place marker and outline it.

With the area marked, we will be removing this area so that the marker will be flush with the back of the Santa.

Start by making a pear cut along the edge of the blank. You will be rounding off both sides of this piece the same amount.

One end of the place marker needs to be tapered down to the thickness shown, which is just under an 1/8". This end will be used to mark the pages of a book.

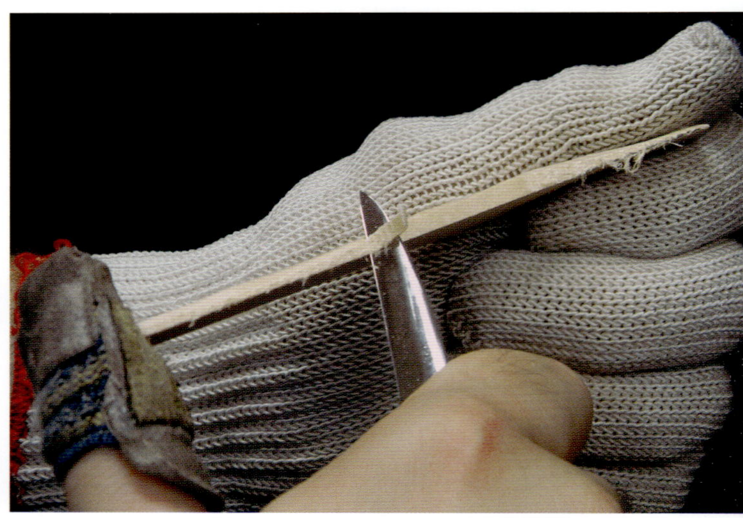

Continue to work the piece down to a thickness that you like. Keep in mind that this will need to fit into a book without being too thick.

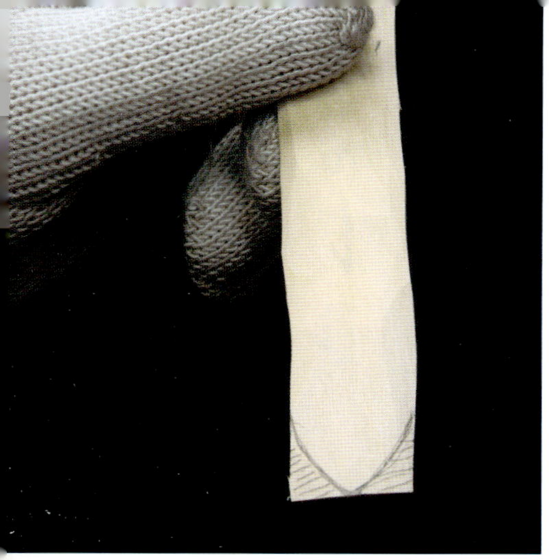

Now, taper the thin end of the place marker so that it is not perfectly square. You can make this completely round or just clip off the corners. I have marked the shaded areas for this one to be removed.

Push cut back towards the top of the line marked. Repeat this process for the other side and the top, removing the wood down to the thickness of the place marker.

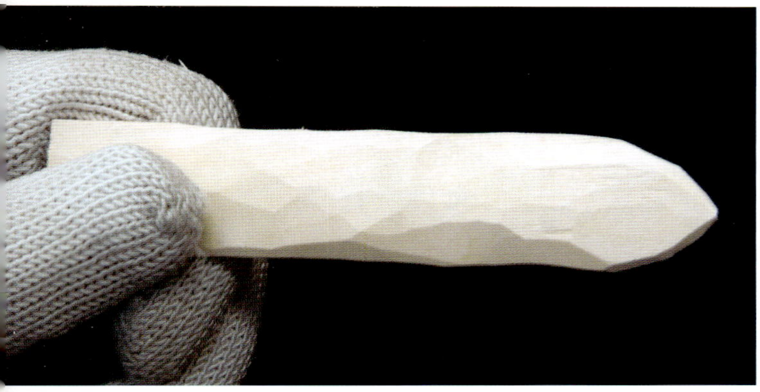

Our completed place marker. Notice the square end — this will be attached to the bookmark.

Now we are ready to fit the place marker.

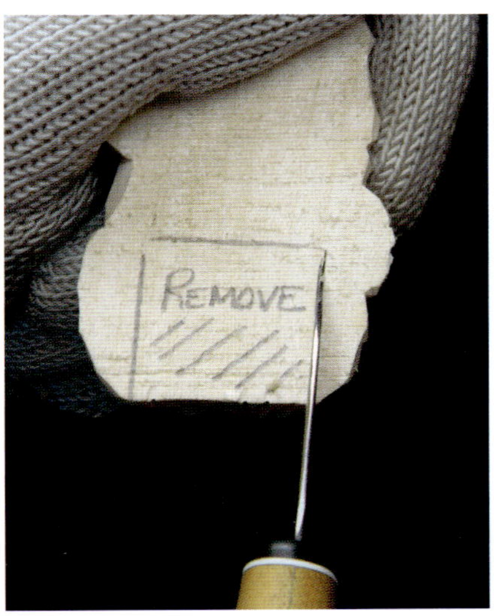

Make a stop cut on the side of the area to be removed. Make this cut fairly deep.

When checking the fit of the place marker, you may need to trim some more of the area inside to get the marker to fit flush with the back of the Santa.

Push cut along the area of the stop cut and remove the piece of wood.

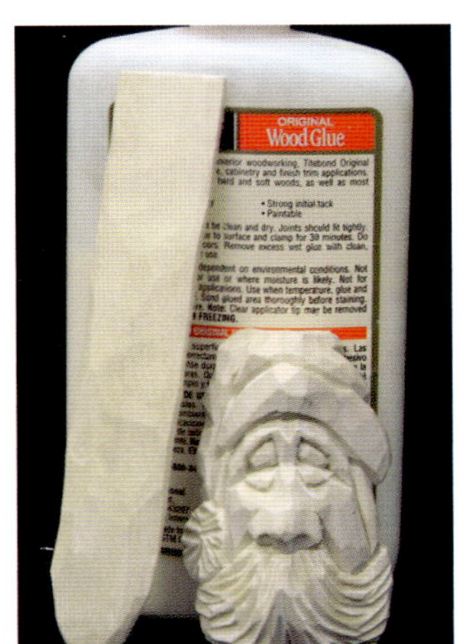

With the place marker fitting good, it is now time to glue it all together.

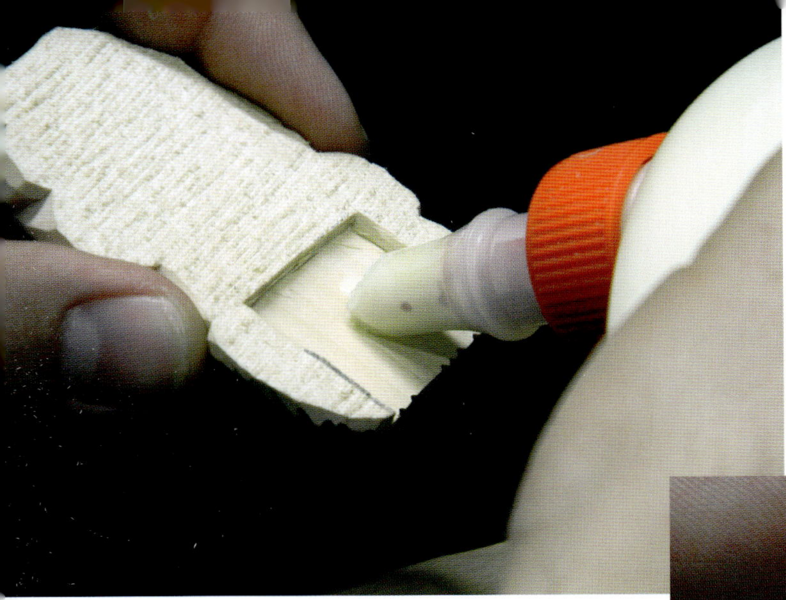

Apply the glue to the area we removed. Make sure to cover the entire area so that we get a good bond with no extra glue coming out the sides.

Nice fit with no excess glue squeezing out.

Clamp the piece together and let it dry for a few hours. We now have a completed piece and will paint the Santa in Chapter 6.

Chapter 6

Painting the Santa Bookmark

Now it is time to paint the Santa bookmark. There are a few items that you will need to paint this bookmark: small and medium size paint brushes, a container of water to wash your brushes in, a small pump spray bottle or container of water big enough to wet your carving, and a paint tray or piece of glass to mix your paints. I prefer a piece of glass to mix my paints on so I can control how thin or thick my colors are. We will be using the following color of acrylic paints: white, red, red oxide, yellow ochre, brown, and black.

For obtaining the right consistency of paint color and the antique solution to be applied after the painting has dried, as well as discarding the materials, refer to the instructions in Chapter 4: Painting the Book Bookmark.

We have our colors on the palette: Yellow Ochre, Red Oxide, White, and Red.

Wet the piece before painting it using a spray bottle.

The piece should be wet, but *not* dripping with water before we apply the paint.

Add a few drops of water and mix the Yellow Ochre and Red Oxide together to make the flesh tone.

With the flesh color mixed, add water to make it a fairly thin color.

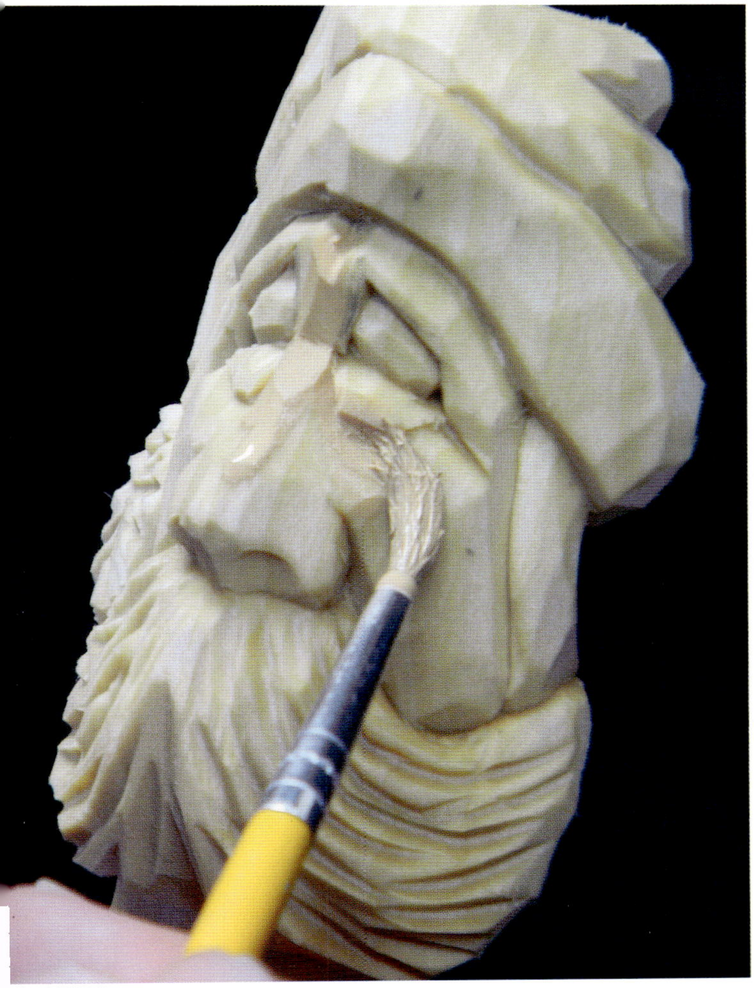

Start applying the flesh color to the face of the Santa covering the eyes.

One half of the face painted.

Paint along the bottom of the cheeks, but make sure not to paint the mustache.

With the face completely painted, check it for even coverage and touch up any areas that you missed.

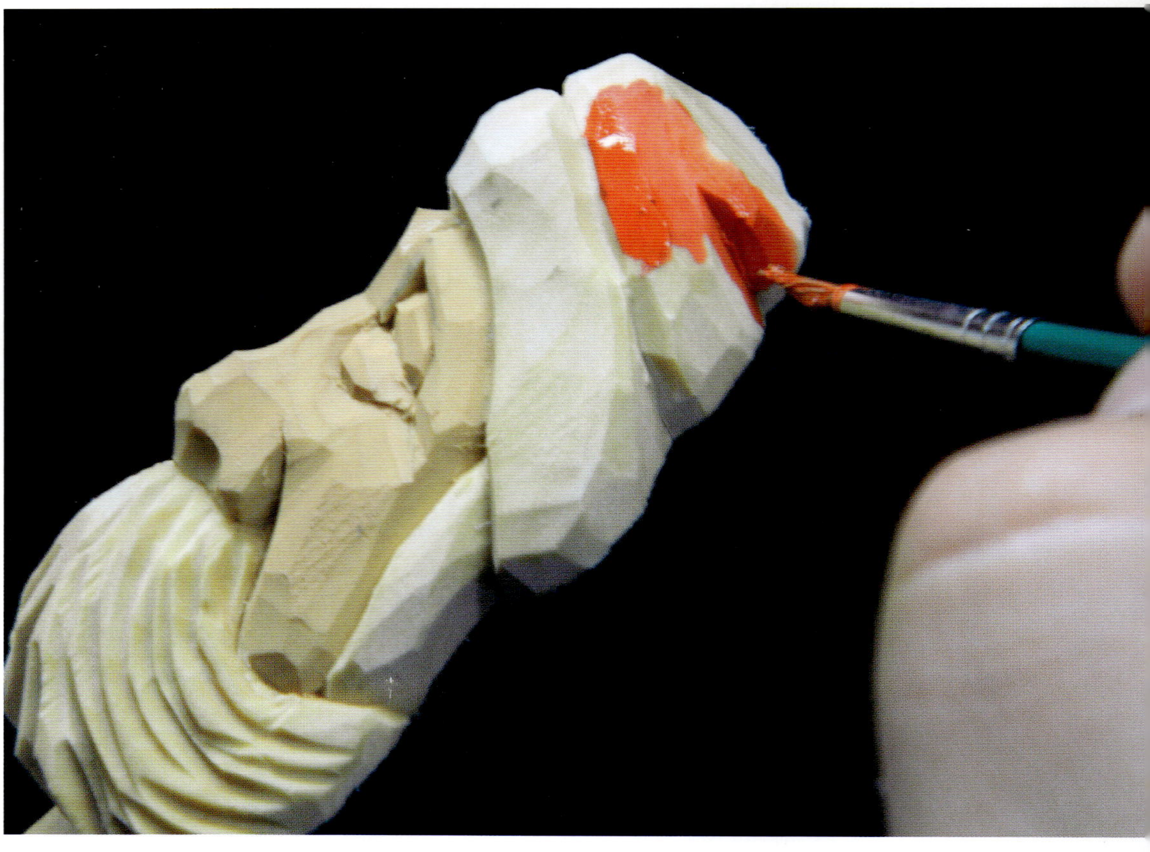

With the Red color, start painting the hat. Avoid contact with the brim.

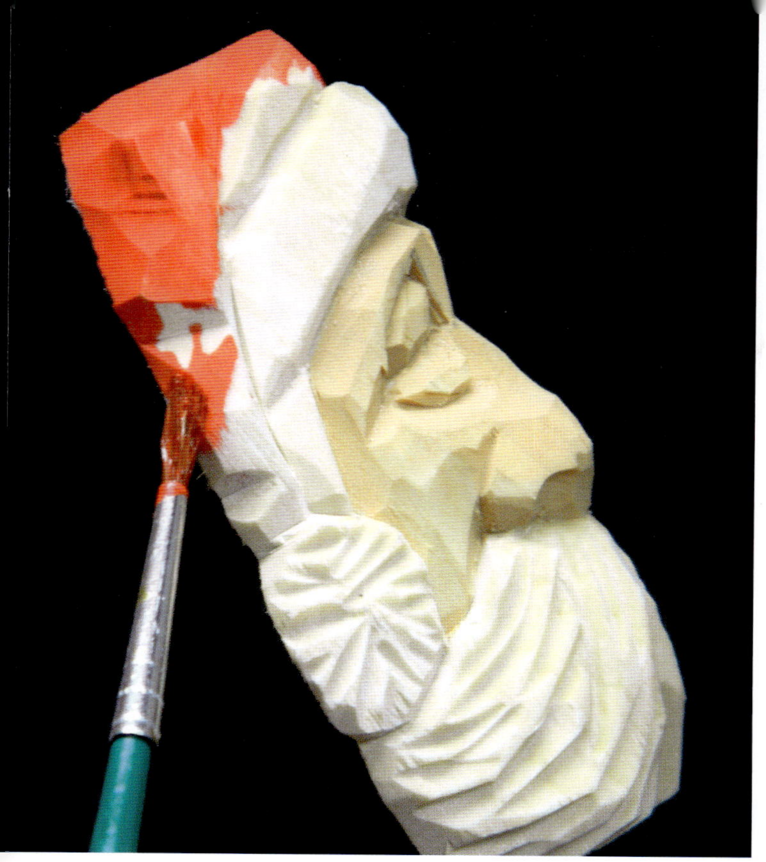

Paint the side of the hat stopping at the ball.

Looking good so far; now paint the mustache.

The face and hat are painted.

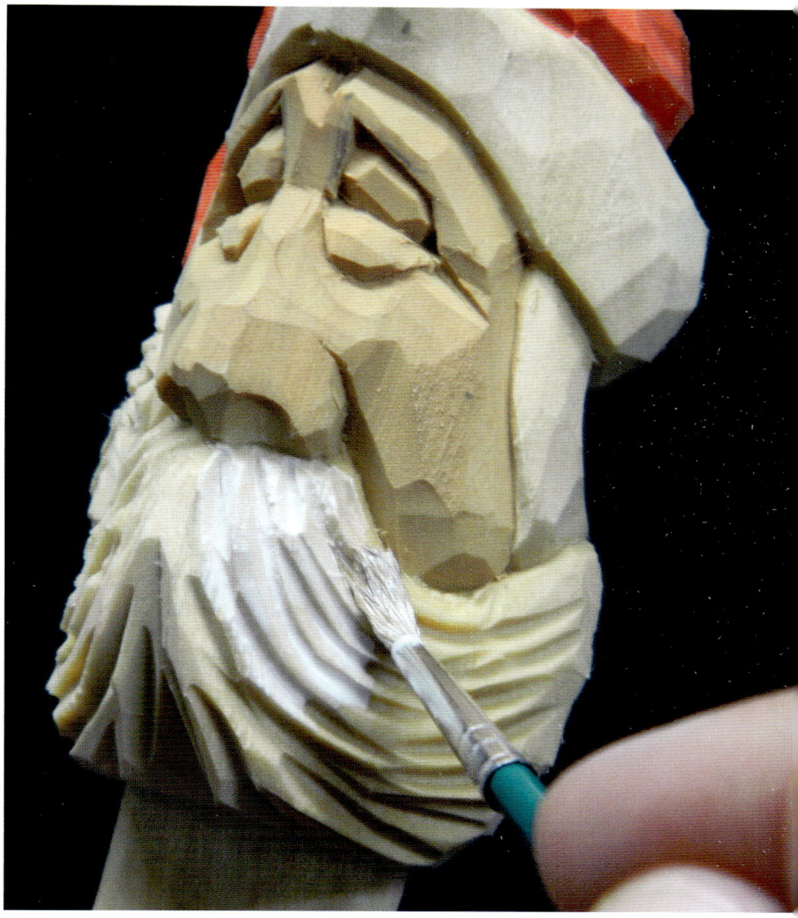

Apply a thinned White paint to the mustache area. Start at the bottom of the nose area and work down the mustache.

One half done; now you can paint the other side.

The mustache is completed.

Paint the ball of the hat with a non-thinned white paint.

Paint the brim and sides of the hair with the non-thinned white paint.

Face, hat, and mustache are now done.

With a smaller brush, paint the eyes using a non-thinned white paint. Take your time painting these areas.

Both eyes are now painted. It may be necessary to apply two coats of paint to get the eyes white.

Add a drop of brown to the palette and use the end of a paintbrush to add the eye color.

With some paint on the handle of the brush, I line up where I want the Santa to be looking and apply the dot of paint to the eye.

The eye color is now applied. Make the dot an appropriate size for the eye.

Both of the eyes have the brown color applied. Next, add a drop of black to the palette to paint the center of the eye.

I use a toothpick to paint the center of the eye. I cut off one end and dip it in the black paint and apply it to the brown color on the eye.

Now dot the other side with the black.

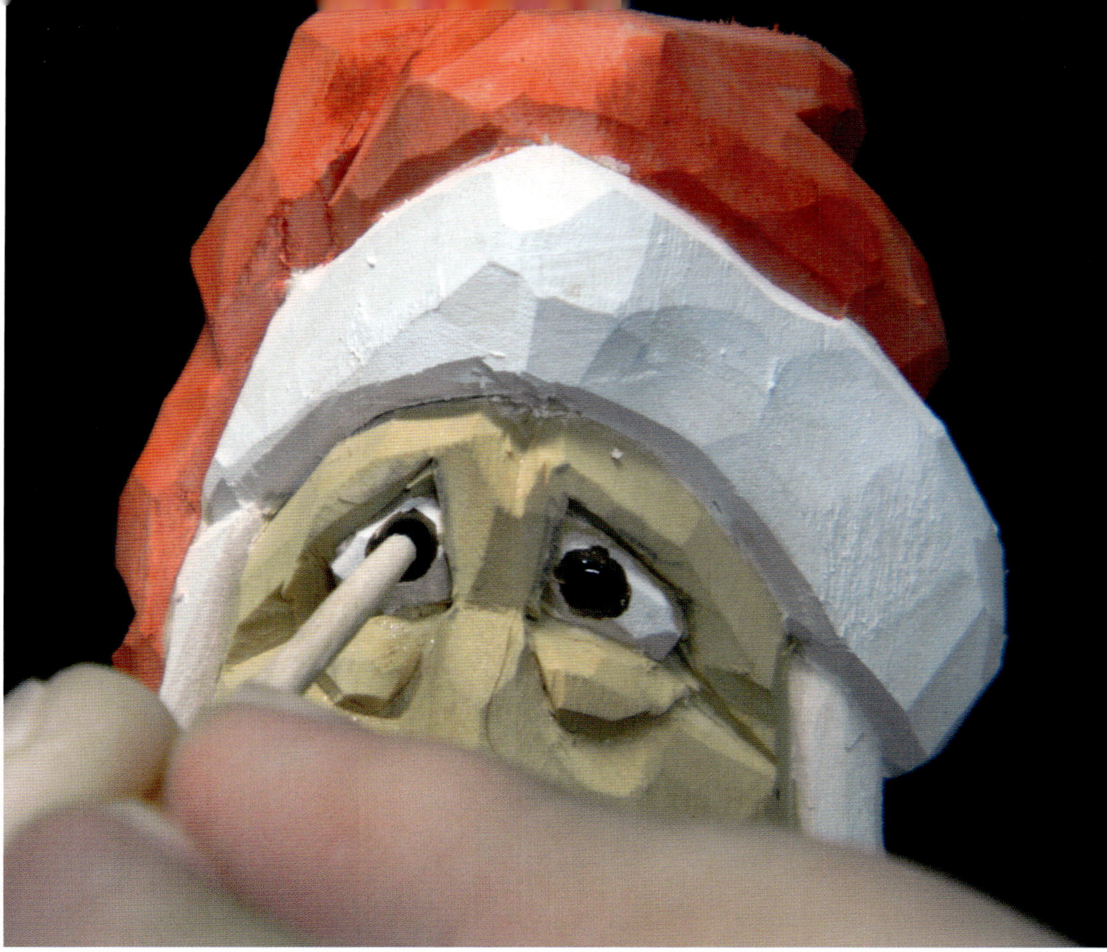

Both eyes are completed. With the non-thinned white color, take the other end of your toothpick and dip it into the white paint.

Apply a small white dot to the black dot to make Santa's eye stand out.

The eyes are now done and look good. Let the piece completely dry before applying the antique.

Dip one half of the bookmark into the antique solution.

One half done, it should be fully covered.

Dip the other half.

Wipe off any excess solution.

Get the solution out of the cuts of the mustache with a paper towel or white shop towel.

There you go: A nice Santa bookmark that any book lover will enjoy!

Patterns and Gallery

Here are just a few of the bookmarks that I have done for various friends and family members. The nice thing about the caricature carvings is they can be as funny and crazy as you like. The best way to get some good faces is to study people and cartoon characters. You will be amazed at the faces that people make and the ideas that will come from those faces. Enjoy the carvings and good luck.

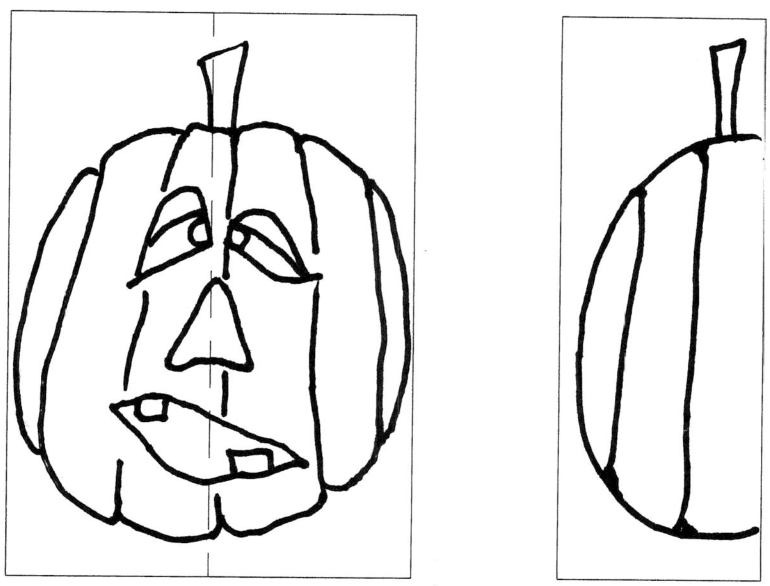

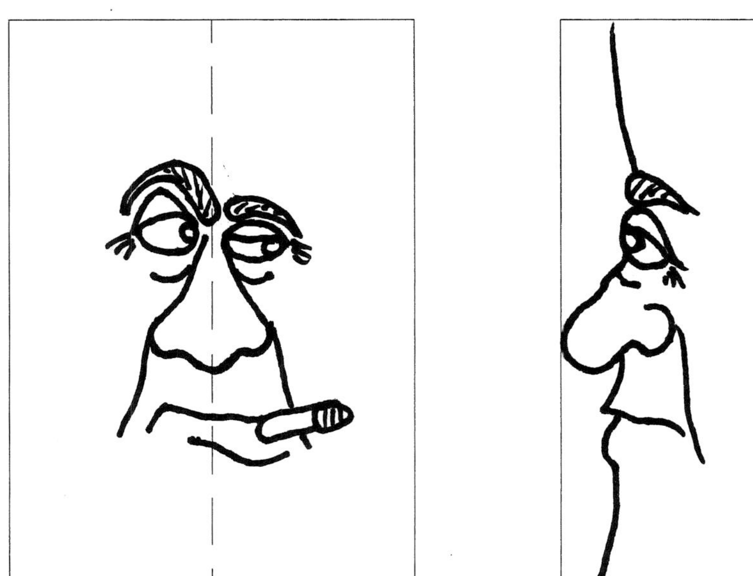